Women and the New Testament

Women and the New Testament

An Analysis of Scripture in Light of New Testament Era Culture

by

Lesly F. Massey

McFarland & Company, Inc., Publishers
Jefferson, North Carolina, and London

Scripture taken from the *New American Standard Bible,* © 1960, 1962, 1963, 1968, 1971, 1972, 1973, 1975, 1977 by the Lockman Foundation. Used by permision.

British Library Cataloguing-in-Publication data available

Library of Congress Cataloguing-in-Publication Data

Massey, Lesly F., 1946–
　Women and the New Testament.

　Bibliography: p. 137.
　Includes index.
　1. Women — Biblical teaching.　2. Women in Christianity — History — Early church, ca. 30–600. 3. Jesus Christ — Views on women.　4. Bible.　N.T. — Criticism, interpretation, etc.　I. Title.
BS2545.W65M37　1989　225.8'3054　　89-42735

ISBN 0-89950-438-8 (lib. bdg. : 50# alk. paper)

Printed in the United States of America

McFarland & Company, Inc., Publishers
　Box 611, Jefferson, North Carolina 28640

To Margaret
for eternal support, patience and love

Contents

Introduction

The status of women has been a source of controversy throughout history. Only in the present century have women begun to enjoy a station which approaches equality with men, and even this is largely limited geographically to North America and parts of Euro-Asia. In the Orient, as in most Islamic and third world countries, antiquated traditions prevail in which women are viewed as ontologically inferior to men and are restricted to a subordinate role.

In all societies the status of women seems integrally linked to religion. Even in the Christian west, where female elevation has been most prominent, there is continual debate among religious leaders as to what limitations should be enforced on change. Some Christian denominations and sects, especially those with a more conservative philosophy, hold tenaciously to the traditional subservience of women, excluding them as a class from positions of clerical authority. Some even formally oppose women holding responsible positions in business or politics, contending that the female's place is in the home, where she should maintain a posture of quiet subjection to her husband's authority.

From both an internal and external vantage point, the obvious conflict between such views and those self-evident ideals characteristic of spiritual maturity seriously damages the credibility of the Bible and Christianity in general. This is unfortunate and cannot be taken lightly.

But there is no easy solution. The Judeo-Christian world embraces a plethora of diverse sects and doctrines, all mutually exclusive and contradictory. And the typical resolution for doctrinal conflict is formal debate and apologetics, each group searching the scriptures for a plausible defense for its beliefs. Unfortunately proof-text theology often blinds us to underlying principles and spiritual truths which form the heart of sacred scripture. Pride, prejudice, tradition, misguided zeal and impenetrable socio-ethnic barriers easily sterilize scripture by predetermining what the reader will understand it to teach before he reads a single verse.

This is also true of *a priori* reasoning concerning the definition, nature

1

and extent of biblical inspiration. Often students of the Bible are pro-
grammed by their teachers to reach certain doctrinal conclusions simply by
unknowingly assimilating their attitudes and presuppositions. And in
many situations teaching the word involves outright indoctrination in
specific and well-defined beliefs which in reality represent an excessively
biased point of view.

But perhaps the most common error in interpretation of scripture is the
failure to appreciate the immediate problems addressed by a biblical writer,
and to give due attention to the dynamics of cultural milieu. Proper biblical
hermeneutics demands that all commands, instructions and implications be
examined in light of the original cultural framework for the writer's terminology and message, and whatever practical application is to be made must
rest on that broad and realistic base. Binding fundamental adherence to instructions taken out of context and developing rigorous church dogma on
the basis of vague historical records is ludicrous.

Yet such has been the case with many church doctrines, both Catholic
and Protestant. And such has been the traditional interpretation of the Bible concerning women.

Women and the New Testament is a reexamination of the New Testament teaching on the status of women, giving careful attention to social and
cultural backgrounds. The world into which the Christian church was born
was a welter of conflicting customs, and the peak of a social crescendo
beginning perhaps two thousand years earlier. The history of the Jews, contained in part in the Old Testament, provides the principal framework for
the establishment of Christianity and reveals substantial influence from
early Egyptian and Babylonian cultures in turn. Greco-Roman culture is
readily visible throughout the New Testament.

Clearly Christianity did not arise in a vacuum, nor did New Testament
spokesmen utter divine oracles totally unrelated to the problems and needs
of their contemporaries. It would appear, in fact, that many customs
established in antiquity survived and developed into those prevalent in the
first Christian century, and are taken for granted by various New Testament writers without any purposeful prophetic endorsement.

As Christianity developed, the apostles and church leaders were
forced to respond to many stressful situations, and much of their organiza-
tional structure and format arose out of necessity. The early church found
itself caught between the ridicule of philosophical conceit and the fires of
persecution. While their beliefs were somewhat revolutionary, Christians
sought diligently not to give cause for offense but to be all things to all people, in the sense of being at peace with everyone and not creating a point
of debate over customs and opinion. This was a hard lesson for Christians
of both Jewish and Gentile extraction, but the end was the peaceful blending of cultures into a united spiritual body.

To accomplish that, much of the apostolic teaching pertained to the sacrifice of self and the spirit of surrender to authority, even to oppressive rulers. These teachings are quite clear with regard to the Roman government, social injustice and slavery. But they are also evident concerning the issue at hand.

Generally those statements in the New Testament which appear to place either religious or social restrictions on women were not intended as universally binding divine mandates, but were simple acknowledgments of or comments concerning the way things happened to be by way of centuries of cultural development and human tradition. These passages must be interpreted in light of the immediate cultural climate and in harmony with the transcendent and ubiquitous spirit of Jesus Christ.

The New Testament, in particular the Gospel accounts of Jesus' ministry, provides a revolutionary doctrine of liberation for women from the degradation and inferiority which they have suffered for millennia. Its principles provide the means whereby the social status of women can be, and has been to a significant degree, elevated wherever it finds receptive minds. And most important to theology, the New Testament as a whole provides for total intrinsic equality among races, classes and sexes, thereby granting to women equal opportunity for service in the kingdom of God.

1. Jesus and Women

Jesus Christ was born and reared a Palestinian Jew in an era deemed by biblical writers a propitious time for the appearance of the Messiah. Judaism had recovered from its fragmentation during and following the Babylonian Exile. Israel had reconstructed her cities; restored her farmlands, economy and social traditions; and, most significant, reinstated temple worship and renewed allegience to the Law of Moses. Yet in the two centuries prior to the birth of Jesus, Israel had experienced much political and social turmoil. She had been ruled by pagan overlords with little sympathy for her customs and faith; first the Greeks, then the Egyptian Ptolemies and Syrian Seleucids, both Greek in culture, and then the Romans. Her religious tradition had suffered division into left- and right-wing factions, and each year scores of her population had abandoned their temple and homeland for residence abroad, satisfied with a substitute worship in the synagogue. Jews of the Diaspora significantly outnumbered Palestinian Jews, and resultingly their identity was threatened by internal and external pressures at every social level.

Palestine lay at the crossroads of trade between the East, West and South, and had become a cosmopolitan complexity unparalleled throughout the world. Recurring insurrection by Jewish nationalists made Palestine a turbulent area demanding strict control by the Roman government.

Into this setting came Jesus of Nazareth. It is certain that the background to the New Testament teaching on the status of women includes, and perhaps climaxes in, the attitude of Jesus toward women. New Testament writers claim Christ as their authority, either by recollection of his teachings and deeds, or by response to inspiration. The New Testament church claims him as its founder and author, and the source of its religious doctrines and way of life. Therefore, whatever status women may have occupied in the early church, and continue to occupy in the church today, should ideally have its roots in the attitude, example and teaching of Jesus in anticipation of a community of believers perpetuating the Gospel after his departure. The Christian Church without a doubt is the direct outcome of the life and ministry of Jesus Christ.

I. JESUS AS A SOCIAL REFORMER

Scholars are in general agreement with regard to the intended influence of Christ's ministry upon society, but Jesus was neither a zealot nor a political rebel. He taught that his kingdom is not of this world and that his disciples should pay taxes and render unto Caesar that which is Caesar's.

Jesus cannot be thought of as a religious reformer. Although he pointed out the hypocrisy among religious leaders and the vanity of legalism and impractical dogma, he was not concerned with reforming Judaism. His aim was to establish a completely new doctrine and a new kingdom, founded upon a new covenant, new sacrifice and new priesthood with new and better promises.

Neither was Jesus an ascetic. Some have attempted to identify him with the Essenes, claiming that his doctrine and healing techniques were learned from that austere Jewish sect. But there is far too much about the ministry of Christ which differs from Essene doctrine for this theory to have merit. There is every possibility that Jesus came in contact with this group, as he did with the Pharisees, Sadducees, Zealots and Herodians, but it is clear that his doctrines were inspired and his works miraculous.

More appropriately, Jesus might be described as a religious and social revolutionary, with a revolutionary message and mission. Early in his ministry Jesus walked into the synagogue of Nazareth, where he was reared, and opening the scroll of Isaiah read:

> The Spirit of the Lord is upon me, because he anointed me to preach the gospel to the poor. He has sent me to proclaim release to the captives, and recovery of sight to the blind, to set free those who are downtrodden, to proclaim the favorable year of the Lord.[1]

After returning the scroll to the official, Jesus sat down and declared, "This day is the scripture fulfilled in your ears." This, indeed was the revolutionary manner of Jesus. His nature was pacifistic, his methods were extraordinary, and his objectives were universal and dynamic. He spoke out against social injustice and moral evil of every description, but avoided the cynicism and recalcitrant spirit of philosophers and rebels of his day. He despised exploitation of the poor in the name of justice which had characterized nobility for centuries, and lashed out far more harshly at religious hypocrisy than at the sins of the common people. Yet so approachable was he that little children could nestle in his arms, and publicans and harlots could venture to embrace him.

Rauschenbush describes Jesus as the builder of a new society, founded on the principle of fellowship and social harmony.[2] As human life originates in love, so love holds together the basal human organization, the family. Contrary to the principles of the social gospel Jesus did not seek to change the structure and nature of society in order to reach individuals, but conversely to change society by changing the hearts and lives of individuals. Matthew speaks of fraternity instructed by Jesus as the functional principle of love towards mankind. He further asserts that the times and places where people "have come most under the influence of the words and life of Jesus have been those in which institutions at variance with fraternity; branding, polygamy, the exposure of children, slavery, drunkenness and licentiousness — have disappeared."[3]

To this very end Jesus labored. The undergirding of his redemptive sacrifice was the establishment of a potential lifestyle whereby the principles of sacrificial love might abolish social injustice. True greatness, Jesus taught, could not be obtained through military conquest, financial gain or social subjugation, but through individual humility and service to others. Cullmann sees this principle at work in the lives of early Christians, and the means whereby the example of Christ continued to influence the world after his departure.[4] For precisely these reasons women held a position of high esteem in the life and ministry of Jesus.

Historical witness to the degraded status occupied by women in most cultures of Christ's day is irrefutable. And the typical morning prayer in which a Jewish male thanked God that he had not been born a Gentile, a slave or a woman, depicts clearly the plight of those women with whom Jesus came in direct personal contact.

Most certainly, in whatever sense, Jesus hoped to provide citizenship to the Gentiles, who were aliens and strangers from the commonwealth of Israel, to set at liberty the captives, to heal the brokenhearted and to give sight to the blind, so he came to liberate women. Holley words it succinctly:

In Jesus' actions and attitudes, in his willingness to come up against the traditions of cultures, in his loving concern, he was revealing the will of God.... Jesus treated women of whatever sort as persons of value and worth, as genuine human beings, not just as inferior or despised females. There was never in his manner any condescending, sentimentalizing, jeering, patronizing or putting them in their place.[5]

Daniel-Rops says that "toward women Jesus always displayed a special kindness" which is worthy of consideration in light of his mission.[6] Pratt says that "women of all ranks in society found in him a benefactor and friend, before unknown in all the history of their sex."[7]

II. WOMEN OF NOTE IN THE LIFE OF JESUS

A great number of women came in contact with Jesus from his childhood through the completion of his ministry. Bible scholars recognize that from the first women were responsive to his teachings and devoted to his person.[8] But for the purpose of Christian theology special attention must be given to those critical yet intimate details which reveal Jesus' true feelings, his deep concerns and his ultimate objectives, both on a spiritual and temporal plane. Herein is to be found the irrefutable premise for Christian doctrine on the status of women.

Mary the Mother of Jesus

An enormous body of myth has been developed concerning the mother of Jesus of Nazareth. Even a shallow glance at the apocryphal legends of Mary's birth and childhood reveals the vivid imagination of ancient hagiographers. *The Protevangelium of James* and the *Gospel of Pseudo Matthew*, both of the third century, name Mary's parents Joachim and Anna, who were supposedly old and beyond hope of bearing children when Mary was conceived. Her birthplace is assigned variously to Sepphoris, Jerusalem and Bethany, and the parents, deciding to dedicate her to God, took her to the temple at the age of three. There she was entrusted to the priests and raised under a vow of chastity, which is impossible to reconcile with Jewish customs of that day. Legend also has the priests holding a contest when Mary is twelve to marry her off and get her out of the temple before the uncleanness of her ensuing menstruation defiled the place. Each contestant was given a stick, and he whose stick first budded and produced leaves won her hand in marriage. The victor was Joseph, a carpenter from Nazareth.[9]

Scholars generally recognize the spurious nature of apocryphal stories concerning Mary, and hold that until her visit by the angel of God she was an obscure peasant girl of Nazareth, a town about which we know nothing, with an unknown and probably uninteresting background. Except for two chapters in Luke and a few verses in the other Gospels and Acts, Mary occupies a place of relative insignificance in the New Testament.

Some authorities see in the mother of Jesus a literary device suggesting that her mention, especially in the Fourth Gospel, serves a symbolic purpose and little else. To others Mary is a genuine figure appearing in historical narratives and whose mention offers brief glimpses into the humanity of Jesus and his attitude toward women as a class. In either case she provides some assistance in establishing the concepts and attitudes which undergird the Christian faith. Therefore the four primary occasions for her mention are significant to the present study.

The Birth and Childhood of Jesus. Mary was no more than twelve to fourteen years of age when she was informed by a heavenly messenger that she would conceive and bear a son, whose name would be Jesus and whom men would call the Son of God.[10] The angel also spoke of Elizabeth's pregnancy, which prompted Mary to journey to the hill country of Judea to visit her kinswoman. The two women were elated at their similar fortune to be selected for an obviously divine service, although Elizabeth acknowledged the superior blessing upon Mary, and the Lukan narrative climaxes in the Magnificat, or hymn of Mary.[11]

The first reaction of the mother of Jesus, however, was one of dismay, for she was a virgin in keeping with the strict norms of Jewish tradition. She was espoused (betrothed) to Joseph, a carpenter of Nazareth, but the marriage had not yet taken place. Since the couple were not permitted to engage in intercourse until after the *huppah*, the second part of the marriage ceremony, Mary's pregnancy indicated her unfaithfulness to her betrothal, a crime punishable by stoning according to tradition. Even if the more severe penalty was waived, Joseph had the right to lodge a virginity suit and divorce his fiancee, freeing himself of all encumbrances of the *ketubbah*. But Matthew suggests that an angel appeared to Joseph informing him that Mary's conception was of the Holy Spirit in fulfillment of prophecy, and in compliance with the vision Joseph took Mary to be his wife and refrained from sexual intercourse with her till after the birth of Jesus.[12]

According to Luke, Joseph was compelled to make a journey from Galilee up to Judea, to Bethlehem the home of his ancestors, to be enrolled according to a general decree of Augustus Caesar.[13] It was there that Mary gave birth to Jesus, and the narrative runs as if she cared for herself, whence the patristic tradition of a painless birth.[14] The inn in which Jesus' parents found no accommodation was probably only a hostel, too crowded by peasant travelers for a birth. The manger where Mary laid her newborn son may have been either a stall, a stable or a cave adjacent to the inn, although some understand it to have been a feeding trough, perhaps in the open air. Regardless of details, the circumstances were humble, to say the least.

Luke relates that shepherds from nearby fields responded to an angelic announcement of the birth and visited Mary, Joseph and the child in their meager accommodations. Matthew mentions nothing of the shepherds, but relates that certain Magi came to Jerusalem seeking information of a new king,[15] after which Herod ordered the massacre of all male infants in the vicinity.[16] Being warned by an angel, Mary and Joseph absconded to Egypt with the child Jesus until they learned of the death of Herod.[17] The Lukan account includes the birth narrative by focusing on the mother: "But Mary kept all these things, pondering them in her heart."[18]

According to Jewish law a mother was required to make an offering at the close of forty days following the birth of a son. Luke's use of a plural

pronoun with reference to the purification is troublesome, in that it implies
a regulation concerning both mother and child. The plural, however, probably represents the writer's blending of two motifs, using Mary's purification simply to introduce the account of Jesus' presentation in the temple.
It is the second motif with which the writer is primarily concerned, evidenced by the finesse with which he draws two aged saints, Simeon and
Anna, into the narrative to hail the advent of God's Messiah.[19] However,
it is interesting to note that the conclusion of Simeon's utterance is addressed to Mary in particular.

When Jesus was twelve, his parents took him back to Jerusalem for the
Feast of the Passover, and in this context Luke relates a further incident in
which Mary plays a prominent role. When the company began their return
home Jesus remained behind in the city, and a day later his parents returned
to look for him. After a three-day search the lad was found "in the temple,
sitting in the midst of the doctors, both listening to them and asking them
questions."[20] It was Mary, according to Luke, who approached Jesus concerning his apparent inconsideration, to which the lad replied: "Why is it
that you were looking for me? Did you not know that I had to be in my
Father's house?" Jesus was not disrespectful in his reply, nor insolent in his
behavior, but was experiencing the increasing awareness of his own divinity and his heavenly commission. The account suggests that he submitted
to his parents' authority, returning to Nazareth at their request where he
continued "increasing in wisdom and stature, and in favor with God and
men." The writer concludes with a second note that Mary "kept all these
sayings" or better "all these things" in her heart. The wording is slightly
different from that of verse 19, but the meaning is essentially the same. The
entire context leaves the impression that Mary fully comprehended the
divine nature of Jesus from the time of his conception, and that she took
careful note of and frequently reflected upon those incidents which gave
testimony to that truth. In fact, the attention given to Mary by the Lukan
author strongly suggests that Mary was a principal source for information
concerning the early life of Jesus. Some feel that if Jesus' mission as the
Messiah had been so well attested as Luke indicates, the negative attitude
of his parents on various occasions is inexplicable. But the periodic doubts
which might naturally arise, and the inability on the part of the parents to
comprehend fully the nature of their son's mission, by no means deny the
possibility of Mary's testimony years later concerning details only she
could know.

The Marriage Feast at Cana. The next chronological appearance of
Mary in the Gospels is at a wedding in Cana of Galilee, attended by Jesus
and his disciples. Mary is identified as the mother of Jesus, her name never
being stated in the Fourth Gospel. The phrase "she was there" does not

indicate her residence in Cana, but merely her presence at the wedding, and it is likely that Mary was an assistant to the host, rather than a guest. The insufficiency of wine might show the family to be rather poor, although it is possible that the feast lasted several days and the quantity of wine required would be difficult to determine beforehand.

The reason for Mary pointing out the insufficiency of wine to her son is unclear. Some feel that she was not necessarily asking for a miracle, but, as in the case of Martha at the death of Lazarus, makes an imprecise suggestion inspired by confidence that Jesus can do something to alleviate the situation. It may be, on the other hand, that Mary would have no reason to approach her son, who was simply a guest at the occasion, unless she recognized in him greater potential than that of an ordinary man. Bultmann, representing scholars who do not regard the story as historically true, says that part of the literary objective of the Evangelist is that Mary called the attention of Jesus to the deficiency explicitly to get him to perform a miracle.[21]

Jesus' answer, "What to me and to you?" seems sharp, abrupt and critical. However, the expression was commonly used in both Jewish and Hellenistic circles to mean very casually "So what?" and displays no harshness or disrespect whatsoever. It is commonly recognized that the term "woman," here used in the vocative, is not as cold and disrespectful as it may sound in English in addressing one's mother. Jesus uses the same expression in his dying hour, when he in tenderness consigns his mother to the guardianship of the beloved disciple. It is very likely that Jesus intentionally selected such a term to emphasize his unique role and the distinction which must exist between physical and spiritual relationships. In his public ministry Jesus was not primarily "the son of Mary" or "the carpenter's son," but rather "the Son of God" and "the Son of Man." Therefore it was important for Mary to grasp that her son was also the Messiah, and she must not presume to direct his affairs.

The answer of Jesus is completed with the statement, "My hour is not come," which surely means "it is not yet time for me to act." There is a remarkable series of passages in John referring to the "hour" of Jesus, the theological implications of which Mary could not have understood at the time.[22] But the apparent aloofness of Jesus in this context can only be explained in connection with the "hour," a time determined by God for a significant act and ultimately to be accomplished in the glorification of Jesus through his Passion.

Mary does not regard her son's words as a direct refusal of the favor she has implied, evidenced by her instructing the servants to do whatever he tells them. The stone waterpots are especially significant in the story, in that they were used for purification purposes and here are worked into the Evangelist's theme of water both in satisfaction of thirst and in purification.[23]

The quality of the wine produced in the miracle story clearly suggests the perfection of life and spirit which the individual can experience through Jesus' ultimate redemptive work. The account closes with a statement that this miracle was Jesus' first, and that it both displayed his glory and produced faith in his disciples.[24] No further mention is made of Mary, or her reaction to the miracle.

It is essential to note that few reputable scholars regard this event as historically credible. It is suggested rather that the Evangelist has here, and in other places in his gospel, drawn upon an early Christian tradition, not as history, but as a literary tool.[25] There can be little doubt but that material throughout the Fourth Gospel is molded in forms based upon current Hellenistic models of philosophy and religious teaching, instead of following the Jewish forms repeated in the Synoptics. In fact, dialogue in John displays striking similarity to the Hermetic dialogues, which follow a long tradition of teaching techniques in the Hellenistic world. However, most of those who deny the historical veracity of the Cana miracle suggest that the story is drawn into the narrative from a tradition or source which antedates the Johannine author and his circle. In this regard Bultmann speaks of a "sign-source," and Schnackenburg discusses a "Cana tradition," utilized by the writer in presenting a preview of Jesus' glory and power, and perhaps as an introduction to his signs. On this basis also, Brown introduces his discussion of the role of women in the Fourth Gospel, suggesting that the Evangelist offers, through discourses constructed from pre-Johannine traditions, "very perceptive corrective . . . to some ecclesiastical attitudes of his (own) time."[26]

A question still arises as to whether the Johannine tradition is not as historically credible as the Synoptic sources, the ultimate problem being the extent to which the author may have modified certain material to suit the literary objectives of his narrative.[27] A general point of agreement among proponents of a Cana tradition is that in the original form there was no response of Jesus such as now appears in 2:4. Here an apparent refusal by Jesus to comply with his mother's suggestion makes the entire story difficult to understand. Brown suggests that the popular picture of Mary's ability as a mother to intervene in Jesus' activities simply did not correspond with the oldest tradition about Jesus' attitude toward his physical family. Therefore, it seems, when the Evangelist inserted the miracle story into his gospel he was careful to modify it by adding 2:4, thus distracting from any notion of Mary's role in the ministry of Jesus.

Ministry at Capernaum. Following the Cana incident, according to the Johannine narrative, Mary, along with Jesus' brothers and disciples, accompanied Jesus to Capernaum, where they took up residence.[28] There Jesus attracted more followers, performed a number of miracles, and engaged in long debates with the Scribes and Pharisees who followed him down from Judea. The synoptists record some interesting details which are best assigned to this period in and around Capernaum, and which offer assistance in understanding Jesus' attitude toward his mother. According to Mark:

> And His mother and His brothers arrived, and standing outside they sent word to Him, and called Him. And a multitude was sitting around Him, and they said to Him, "Behold, Your mother and Your brothers are outside looking for You." And answering them, He said, "Who are My mother and My brothers?" And looking about on those who were sitting around Him, He said, "Behold, My mother and My brothers!" For whoever does the will of God, he is My brother and sister and mother."[29]

On this occasion Jesus was seated within a house surrounded by his disciples and others who were interested in his teaching, and, according to Mark, was in the process of defending himself against the accusation of the Scribes that his powers could be attributed only to Satan. Earlier his family had become concerned about his behavior and had at least once attempted to take him into custody, thinking him to be mad. But his discourse was interrupted by a message, no doubt passed through the crowd orally, from his mother and brothers. It is probable that in the thinking of his audience common piety demanded that Jesus respect the request of his mother. However, Jesus was aware of his brothers' disbelief, and he knew, even from scripture, that there were occasions in which the will of God took precedence over family ties. Therefore, his reaction was to dismiss his personal relationship with his family, and draw attention to deeper spiritual relationships attainable by compliance with the will of God. Jesus displayed no contempt for his mother, or for family relationships in general, but, as was the case in the temple when he was a lad and at the marriage feast in Cana, he refused to allow his family to distract attention from the vital features of his ministry. Elsewhere in the Synoptics Jesus is reported to have instructed that anyone who allows father, mother, brother or sister to take priority over the will of God is unworthy of the kingdom.[30] On one occasion during his ministry an unnamed woman cried out in praise, "Blessed is the womb that bore You, and the breasts at which You nursed." Immediately Jesus turned attention from any physical parentage, and focused upon obedience to divine will: "On the contrary, blessed are those who hear the word of God, and observe it."[31]

At the Cross and After the Resurrection. Only the Fourth Gospel includes the mother of Jesus among those women who accompanied him to the cross and remained with him till his death.[32] More significant, it is this very account which gives the only clear picture of a tender and affectionate attitude of Jesus toward his mother.

In the company of Mary Magdalene, Mary the wife of Clopas, and several others, the mother of Jesus drew near to the cross after it had been erected and fixed in place. At that particular time Jesus was fully conscious, and capable of observing his surroundings and speaking. Although the Evangelist depicts a critical moment — Jesus experiencing the agony of the cross — he is careful to portray a human side of Jesus nowhere else so clearly noted. Jesus gazed down at his mother and realized the mental agony she must be experiencing. He also thought of the loneliness which she would suffer in the days ahead and therefore took the opportunity to attend to a last filial duty in compliance with the Fourth Commandment to honor father and mother. The details and significance of Jesus' act, however, are uncertain. Jesus, being the eldest son of Mary, was her legal guardian, assuming that Joseph had died, and probably felt a responsibility to consign his mother to the maintenance of another. Traditionally, "the beloved disciple" has been identified as John the son of Zebedee, who also is thought by most to have written the Fourth Gospel as an eyewitness to much that is recorded in it. If the traditional view is correct, one can respect Jesus' choice in view of the lack of faith on the part of his own brothers. Those scholars who question the historicity of much of the material in the Fourth Gospel feel that both the mother of Jesus and the beloved disciple, whose personal names are never used by the Evangelist, serve in this gospel as symbols of discipleship in various circumstances. But the sections of the Fourth Gospel relating to Mary bear all the marks of veracity, and if so offer an interesting glimpse into the personal attitudes of Jesus toward his mother.

The last New Testament mention of Mary is Acts 1:14, where she is in the company of disciples abiding in Jerusalem according to Jesus' instruction before his Ascension. Nothing is known with certainty about her later life, but tradition has her living in Jerusalem with John for eleven years after the death of Jesus, and dying there in her fifty-ninth year.

In brief, the position of Mary in the life of Jesus, and her role in the New Testament, is far from glamorous. She was an ordinary woman, and was subject to all the social regulations incumbent upon Jewish women of her day. Jesus gave her the respect due a mother, but it seems that he made special efforts to disallow her receiving any praise or adoration which might distract from his divine ministry.

The Samaritan Woman

When Jesus concluded the first phase of his Judean ministry, he and his disciples set out for Galilee, taking the shortest route which led through Samaria. The route took the group past Sychar, and while the disciples entered the city to buy food Jesus relaxed by Jacob's well.[33] The Fourth Gospel contains an interesting account of Jesus' encounter with a Samaritan woman in this setting, and the details prove most enlightening with regard to the attitude of Christ toward women.[34]

The first noteworthy feature of the incident is that Jesus spoke to a Samaritan. It is commonly acknowledged that pious Jews of Christ's day avoided all contact with Samaritans, and the woman herself was startled by the unorthodox behavior of the stranger. Various factors contributed to the animosity between the two nations. The beginning of this mutual hatred might be traced to the political split in Israel nine centuries before Christ, which produced the Northern and Southern kingdoms. But a primary cause for the negative attitude toward Samaritans was their impure blood line. Since 722 B.C., when the kingdom of Israel fell to Assyria, the survivors of Israel had interbred with Canaanites and had virtually lost identity with the lineage of Jacob, except by tradition. Another contributing factor was the development of a distinct religious tradition whose center was Mt. Gerizim. This is suggested by the woman herself in asking Jesus concerning the correct place of worship. But regardless of origin, the fact of social and religious animosity between Jew and Samaritan is undeniable.

A second possible social violation on the part of Jesus, perhaps corporate with the first, was that he would converse publicly with a woman. The Jews regarded it inappropriate for a man to address a woman in public, even one's wife, sister or daughter, for fear of scandal. It is difficult to know the extent of this attitude in the time of Christ, but there is ample reason to suspect that his conduct, if observed, would have resulted in more than simply raised eyebrows.

There is also the possibility that the violation involved more than either contact with a Samaritan or conversation with a female, but rather a combination of the two. In this connection note must be taken of the concluding clause of verse 9, where an explanation of the woman's surprise is inserted into the story by the writer, or perhaps by a later copyist. Daube offers an interesting alternative to the traditional translation of the verb *sugchrasthai* and shifts the emphasis of the alleged repugnance felt by Jews from Samaritans in general to Samaritan women in particular. Daube asserts that the true meaning of the term in question is not "to have dealings with," the definition given by lexicographers, but rather "to use together with" in the sense of making use of a utensil in common with another. The passage then would reflect a rabbinical regulation concerning purity founded on the belief that "the daughters of the Samaritans are menstruants from the cradle."[35] Since a Samaritan woman was regarded as unclean at all times any vessel she held or drank from would likewise be rendered unclean. It is this regulation perhaps which Jesus ignored by asking a drink from a vessel carried by a Samaritan woman.

Regardless of the precise nature of Jesus' misconduct in this case, he appears to have held little regard for either rabbinic and social regulations concerning women, or for the traditional contempt for Samaritans. Jesus did forbid his disciples to preach to Samaritans when he sent them on the limited commission.[36] But this prohibition seems to have been determined by expedience, as was the avoidance of ministry to Gentiles, until the appropriate time for universal evangelization. Christ was fully aware that his own redemptive mission included all nations, and he held none of the ethnic and class prejudices typical of his Jewish contemporaries. In fact, of special interest to the Lukan writer is attention given by Jesus to Samaritans, women and other despised classes.[37]

The bulk of the Johannine story of the Samaritan woman hinges on a conversation clearly initiated by Jesus concerning the metaphor of "living water." Here there is a clear thematic link between this story and the preceding sections (viz. Nicodemus and the Cana miracle) by the use of the term "water." The woman's misunderstanding, which also appears to be a literary device to intensify Jesus' self-revelation in verse 26, prompts her to question his implication that he is somehow greater than the patriarch Jacob who dug the well centuries before.

The conversation is redirected by Jesus' command, "Go call your husband." The superficial implication of these words might be that if the woman would bring her husband Jesus could proceed to explain the "living water" concept, her husband being according to contemporary thought, her guardian and her intellectual superior. Whether Jesus was aware of her marital situation by supernatural perception is a moot question, but Bultmann and others acknowledge this to be the impression the Evangelist intended to leave.[38] Some scholars see a sad apologetic note in the woman's reply, "I have no husband." By making no attempt to call the man with whom she was presently living, she revealed an awareness of her illicit behavior and perhaps an attitude of penitence. But others detect an air of flirtation, perhaps revealing a lack of penitence. In either case Jesus' immediate response concerning her five previous husbands suggests the fullness of his perception, and startled the woman to the conclusion that he must be a prophet. The subsequent discussion of true worship led the woman to link the prophet with the contemporary expectance of a Messiah who, she said, "will tell us all things." From a literary standpoint, the entire discourse builds up to this point, at which Jesus revealed his identity with words clearly typical of the "I am" pronouncements in the Fourth Gospel.

The credibility of the story is called in question by certain scholars. Craveri, for example, calls it "a very beautiful tale," but feels certain that it is historically untrue. Strauss, in agreement with the opinions of Heracleon and Origen, gives the story an instructive and allegorical interpretation, and attributes it to an "idealizing biographer." The difficulty, however, cannot by resolved by an analysis of this one story, for the

credibility of all Johannine discourses must be weighed in light of author-
ship and literary purpose of the entire work. And in this regard there is considerable scholastic disagreement. But arguments for some historical tradition behind the Johannine narratives, such as that made by Dodd, make it
difficult to categorically deny their historical veracity. Therefore, it is not
inconceivable that the Samaritan woman with whom Jesus conversed at the
well of Sychar was a genuine figure in history, or that an incident such as
that recorded in John 4 really occurred.[39]

Irrespective of the genuineness of the story, however, the symbolism
to be observed in the role of the Samaritan woman is striking. First, the
story reveals Christ's disregard for nonsensical social taboos and class
distinction. He saw all races and classes of humanity on an equal plane. A
Samaritan woman was as much worthy of Jesus' conversation as a Jewish
rabbi. Second, the discourse and its aftermath reveal the potential in
women as messengers of the will of God and the good news of salvation.
Third, the Evangelist points out that the woman left her waterpot at the
well in order to fulfill a task she regarded as more important. This, as does
the story of Mary and Martha to be discussed later, indicates the
acceptability of women setting aside domestic chores for occasions of
spiritual pursuit. Fourth, it is worth noting that Jesus was not preoccupied
with unraveling the complex sinful state of the woman's life. He did no
more than point it out, and that, so it seems, merely to draw attention to
his supernatural perception. He did not scorn, rebuke or ridicule her. But
the story implies that a change came over the woman's life because she met
Jesus, and she became an instrument of good in ways which may have been
both extraordinary and socially unacceptable in that day.

The Adulterous Woman

The narrative known as the Pericope of the Adulteress, traditionally
located in John 7:53–8:11, is very clearly of non–Johannine origin. Nevertheless, the incident appears to have circulated in certain parts of the
Western church as oral tradition, and was eventually incorporated into
various manuscripts at different places.[40] While the historicity of the story
might be called in question, both on grounds of textual evidence and intrinsic credibility, it cannot be dismissed categorically from the collection of
material pointing to the historical Jesus. The story is undoubtedly of ancient origin, and it bears all the earmarks of historical veracity. For the objectives of the present study the story has a special value, particularly in
revealing the compassion of Jesus for the sinful and the condemned, even
among women.

The sinister motive of the Scribes and Pharisees who brought the
woman to Jesus is pointed out by the writer and is evidenced by the

question put to Jesus placing him in the awkward position of passing judgment upon the woman. While it is true that the Law of Moses required severe punishment for adultery, it is doubtful that the death penalty was frequently or strictly enforced. According to the *Mishnah*, guilty persons were amenable to the extreme penalty only when taken in the very act, and it was recognized that such legal evidence was difficult to obtain.[41] Therefore, the case of a woman caught in the very act of adultery, suggesting that witnesses had seen the couple engaging in intercourse, was both unusual and one for which there would be little hope of avoiding the severest penalty.

It is fruitless to ask what Jesus wrote on the ground. The words were either irrelevant, or had no impact on the group, for they persistently demanded an answer. But it is probable that Jesus' action represents a direct refusal to pronounce judgment, tactfully avoiding being forced into a snare of legal technicality. His eventual answer implies that whoever has offended in one point of the law is guilty of all, and that none of the woman's accusers had a moral right to sit in judgment over anyone. Therefore, his words "cast a stone" upheld the Mosaic law, while the words "without sin" dismissed anyone who dared to apply it.

When the accusers had left the woman standing alone, as if in the center of an arena, Jesus offered clemency in place of the threats of execution she had suffered a few moments earlier. There is no declaration of pardon for sin, as in the case of the penitent woman discussed by Luke,[42] for the woman before Jesus on this occasion came to him under compulsion and condemnation, and displayed no signs of penitence. Here Jesus gave a promise of forbearance, not justification. But the pericope does reveal a striking degree of compassion on the part of Jesus for this unfortunate individual. While his own ministry was jeopardized, he was aware of her embarrassing predicament. He understood the requirements of the Law of Moses, but he was more concerned for her life and was hopeful for her penitence in the future.

Mary and Martha of Bethany

Among the closest of Jesus' friends were two sisters named Mary and Martha, along with their brother Lazarus. Like the unnamed "beloved disciple" these three are described by the writer of the Fourth Gospel as being loved by Jesus in a very deep and special way. They lived in Bethany, a village about two miles from Jerusalem on the road to Jericho, and it would appear that Martha was the eldest and mistress of the household.[43] Jesus' acquaintance with this family was no doubt long-standing, but the Gospels record only three instances in which one or both sisters have contact with him. All three have bearing on his philosophical posture toward women.

A Visit with Mary and Martha. One of those occasions is a visit to their home by Jesus recorded in the Gospel of Luke. Here they are introduced as if unfamiliar both to the writer and his audience, but the tone of the incident leaves the impression that Jesus knew them well.[44] The writer's purpose, it seems, is to contrast mundane and spiritual motivations in individuals, represented by Martha and Mary respectively. Superfluous details are avoided, such as whether the disciples or Lazarus happened to be present, and attention is drawn immediately to the circumstances which facilitate a memorable statement from Jesus. While Martha seemed relentlessly obsessed with preparing food, Mary sat at Jesus' feet totally absorbed by his words. Jesus seemingly did not notice or comment on the difference between Mary and Martha until the latter became impatient with her sister and complained.

The nature of Jesus' response might have been determined by the fact that Martha directed her complaint at him, in a sense rebuking him for his apparent unconcern that she was doing all the work. And no doubt Mary momentarily feared hearing Jesus instruct her to rise up and help her sister. Instead, he took note of Martha's impatience and her excessive concern for the details of hospitality. His rebuke, though mild and controlled, was directed at what he perceived to be "an agitated state of mind" (*merimnas*) and "the outward noise" (*thorubadze*) caused by her excitement.[45]

> Martha, Martha, you are worried and bothered about so many things;
> but only a few things are necessary, really only one, for Mary has chosen
> the good part which shall not be taken away from her.

The full meaning of Jesus' words is difficult to ascertain, although it appears that Martha was going to more trouble than he thought necessary. She was preparing too much food, several courses perhaps, and Jesus considered one to be quite sufficient. He wanted nothing elaborate and was more interested in their company.

In any case, his response contains an obvious compliment for Mary, because her interest in learning or hearing whatever he had to say was greater than her desire to impress and entertain him. However, the one needful thing which Jesus had in mind may have been concern for loftier matters than food, which he saw in Mary and considered praiseworthy. Since we do not know the topic of their conversation it is somewhat presumptuous to credit Mary with greater spiritual depth than Martha, or assume that she was concerned intensely with religious truth and unity with God, "which matters are eternal and would not be taken away by the eroding forces of time." Such is indeed common homiletic application of the story and is reminiscent of the charge in the Sermon on the Mount, "Seek first the kingdom of God and his righteousness, and all these things will be added to you."[46] But this may be crediting the incident with deeper spiritual overtones than it deserves. It is just as likely that Jesus considered conversation with people more valuable and important than food, and refused to deprive Mary of what seemed important to her also.

Of course, it should be remembered that Jesus normally would not have criticized Martha for her extravagance in preparing more than necessary. It was more like him to let her express her love for him in her own way, even if it was too elaborate. But his rebuke was in response to her criticism of Mary. In essence he was saying, "You tend to what you think is important, and allow her the same privilege."

Also of critical importance is the fact that Jesus would be willing to sit in conversation with women in such a manner, or that he might have instructed them privately as a rabbi might instruct a promising student. This very fact, regardless of the spiritual depth of their talk, reveals an attitude toward women which was uncommon among Jews of Jesus' day and reflective of his revolutionary manner. Although some scholars regard this and other dialogues in the Synoptics and the Fourth Gospel as fabricated allegories, there is reason to believe it to be a genuine glimpse into the mind of Jesus and an attempt on his part to lay the groundwork for the elevation of the social status of women through the Gospel message.

The Raising of Lazarus. It might be said that all the critical problems of the Fourth Gospel are summed up in miniature in John 11:1–57, in which is recorded another incident involving Mary and Martha and which may be considered the seventh sign concerning Jesus' divinity. Critics are especially concerned with the absence of such a stupendous miracle from the Synoptics, and generally conclude that the story simply could not be true. Numerous reputable scholars, however, find sufficient basis for accepting its historical veracity.[47] Since the miracles worked around Jerusalem were not included in the Synoptics, for several possible reasons, the absence of the Lazarus story is not surprising. There are in fact two resurrection stories in the synoptic tradition which the Fourth Gospel excludes, and there is little reason to regard one as more dramatic than the others.[48]

The Evangelist makes it clear that Jesus intentionally delayed two full days after learning of Lazarus' sickness, so that his eventual death might serve as an occasion for a demonstration of power. Under the circumstances, naturally, his intentions could not be appreciated fully either by his disciples or the family of Lazarus.

It is noteworthy that when the sisters of Lazarus are introduced in the account the younger sister, Mary, is named first and the Evangelist takes care to identify her as the one who anointed Jesus with ointment.[49] Also, Mary alone is mentioned in verse 45, probably arising from her greater importance in Christian tradition, and from her closer relationship with Jesus.

In contrast, the writer mentions Martha first when describing the love Jesus felt for this family, and it is Martha who went out to meet him when hearing of his approach to Bethany.

When Jesus arrived Lazarus had been in the grave four days. The disappointment felt by the believers among Lazarus' family and friends is clearly expressed in Martha's despondent greeting: "Lord, if You had been here my brother would not have died." But her subsequent statement, although puzzling, reveals a significant degree of faith in Jesus' power and seems to be a direct plea for a miracle. Jesus' response, "Your brother shall rise again," might not have been intended to reveal his intention of resurrecting Lazarus but rather to gradually educate and clarify Martha's faith. The Evangelist may have, at this point, credited Martha with more than she actually said, for her almost disappointed reference to the resurrection at the last day perfectly sets the stage for Jesus' declaration in verses 25–26:

> I am the resurrection and the life; he who believes in Me shall live even
> if he dies, and everyone who lives and believes in Me shall never die.

Martha's confession of Christ as the Son of God, subsequent to the above-mentioned pronouncement, is probably the closest parallel to Peter's noted confession as may be found anywhere in the New Testament, and it is especially significant that the Evangelist attributes this testimony to a woman.[50] This fact, coupled with Jesus' conversation with Martha concerning the resurrection, the central message of the Gospel, illustrates both the noble status women occupied in the mind of Jesus and the recognition of that fact by the writer of the Fourth Gospel.

Mary's role in the Lazarus story is also interesting, though not of the same nature as the role of Martha. While the older sister serves as an intellectual interlocutor, Mary is a crucible for emotion and compassion. She is credited with a statement of disappointment similar to that of her sister: "Lord, if You had been here, my brother would not have died." But the Evangelist pictures Mary as kneeling in tears at Jesus' feet, surrounded by friends mourning the loss of their friend Lazarus.

Jesus' reaction to these dismal circumstances, described by the writer in the simple words "Jesus wept," is the subject of considerable interest on the part of scholars. It is certain that Jesus did not mourn for the dead Lazarus, but rather in sympathy for those who suffered the loss and whose faith was insufficient to destroy grief through trust in the power he was about to display.

Mary and Martha are significant in this Gospel narrative in that they were among the few to witness Jesus shedding tears. But more important, their personalities serve as instruments in the circumstances climaxing in a most dramatic display of Jesus' power over death.

Mary Anoints Jesus with Oil. Shortly after the raising of Lazarus and just six days before Passover, according to the Fourth Gospel, Jesus attended a supper in Bethany.[51] Martha served the meal, and Lazarus was present reclining with Jesus as they ate. At some point a woman whom the writer clearly identifies as Mary took a bottle of expensive ointment and anointed the feet of Jesus, wiping them with her hair. Judas Iscariot began to complain that the ointment could have been sold for three hundred denarii, almost a year's wage for a laborer of that day, and given to the poor. But Jesus insisted that she be left alone, attributing to her gesture an anticipation of the day of his burial.

Similar stories are recorded in all three Synoptics, though considerable complications arise in attempting to harmonize the details. This is of course a part of a scholastic puzzle commonly called "the Synoptic Problem," which involves explaining all the similarities and differences between Matthew, Mark and Luke. On this particular incident some conclude a separate anointing for each record, while others hold to one anointing the details of which have been garbled and transmitted in various forms. Most commentators distinguish only two anointings, an approach which does the most justice to all accounts. Matthew, Mark and the writer of the Fourth Gospel all agree that the incident occurred in the town of Bethany toward the close of Jesus' ministry, that complaints arose concerning the waste of expensive ointment, that Jesus defended the woman by contrasting the perpetual plight of the poor with his own temporary physical presence, and that Jesus saw in the anointing a preparation for his burial. Therefore, it is plausible that these three writers drew upon a single historical incident involving Mary of Bethany, whereas Luke's story centers upon a different woman and a different occasion.

The significance of the anointing by Mary is also debatable. Even if this woman remains unidentified, the love and devotion she felt for Jesus remain strikingly characteristic of Mary. Here one must note that Jesus openly condoned the extravagance necessitated by an impulse of love. But the consistency of the three records in pointing toward Jesus' burial might indicate the woman's keener awareness of the Lord's impending fate than that possessed even by his chosen twelve. None of them would accept that he must be crucified to fulfill his purpose, even in the closing hours of his life, and there is no indication that on this occasion they comprehended his allusion to death. It is possible that she did more than she realized, and if Matthew and Mark are correct in stating that she poured the ointment on his head, Christ may have regarded the incident as a symbolic anointing to the spiritual offices of prophet, priest and king. If such was the case, Mary's humble and obscure ministry to Christ must be regarded as highly significant, for she officiated in a great ceremony of ordination, perhaps even preparing Jesus for his triumphal entry into Jerusalem.

The Sinful Woman Who Anointed Jesus

Luke records another occasion on which Jesus was anointed by a woman. While numerous scholars contend that the four Gospels contain records of a single incident with details garbled, it is quite clear that Luke has preserved an independent story.[52] This occasion is likewise a dinner, but the writer identifies the host as Simon the Pharisee and places the incident in Galilee early in the Lord's ministry. The atmosphere of the meal is far from pleasant, in that the host and his friends have invited Jesus primarily for the purpose of questioning him concerning his doctrine, and few if any of those at the table are Jesus' disciples. The Lukan writer does not identify the woman with Mary of Bethany, whom he and the Fourth Evangelist are certain to have known well.[53] Instead, he calls her "a woman of the city, a sinner," leaving the impression that she is a street prostitute and perhaps notorious in her community. Surprise at her uninvited appearance is expressed in the writer's exclamation, "And behold a woman." The *alabastron* which she carried was a stone flask containing *muron*, an expensive and strongly aromatic perfume. The writer is careful to state that the woman stood at Jesus' feet behind him, weeping, and that she wet his feet with her tears, wiped them with her hair, kissed them and then anointed them with the ointment.

Unlike the story included in John and the other two Synoptics, however, there is no criticism from Judas or Jesus' disciples about the waste of expensive ointment. Instead, attention is focused on the Pharisee who hosted the occasion, who thought to himself that if this man were a prophet surely he would know what kind of woman he was permitting to touch him. Jesus was not a frequent visitor to the homes of Pharisees, for they knew him to keep the company of publicans and sinners with whom the pious would not associate. Perhaps for this reason the customary courtesies of foot washing and anointing extended to guests were ignored on this occasion, as was the kiss of fellowship, as a deliberate indication of Simon's disrespect for Jesus. But Jesus did not mention the matter till Simon and his Pharisee friends displayed their disapproval of his accepting the gestures of a disreputable woman. The narrative presents Jesus as dealing with the problem by relating a story of two debtors, illustrating gratitude for forgiveness, and by this means Simon was given occasion to rethink his position.

Without question, the account portrays Jesus as accepting the woman's act of love and kindness as evidence of penitence for much sin, and pardon is extended on the basis of faith. The Pharisee, whose outward sins may have been few, had not understood the basic thrust of the Messianic mission: to meet human need at its deepest level and to give peace, freedom and forgiveness to the worst of sinners, even to a prostitute.

Woman with a Hemorrhage

A pericope found in all three Synoptics gives a further glimpse into the attitude of Christ toward women. While Jesus was in the region of Decapolis, he was accosted by hordes of people who clamored about him because of his fame as a healer. Among them was a woman who had suffered an issue of blood for twelve years.[54] The Markan account states that she had "suffered many things from many physicians, and had spent all that she had" seeking a cure, but her ailment had only grown worse.

Rabbinical tradition offers numerous popular remedies of the day. One was to have the woman sit at the fork of two roads holding a vessel of wine, and a physician would approach her from behind and cry out to the flow of blood to cease. Another was to force the patient to swallow a grain of barley from the stable of a white mule. This particular malady was one which not only brought the woman much discomfort and inconvenience, being a perpetual state of uterine hemorrhage, but one which had rendered her ceremonially impure by Jewish law for a total of twelve years.[55] Having exhausted her finances in seeking a cure, her timid approach to Jesus, perhaps in fearful anxiety, appears to be her last hope.

The woman knew that her state was one of uncleanness and that to touch a Jewish male, or to be touched by him, while in this state was forbidden. Tradition held that if a man forgot some jars in the courtyard, even though they had tightly fitting covers, he deemed them unclean, lest they had been moved or touched by a menstruant woman and he thereby be defiled. Some have suggested that it is unlikely that a pious Jew of Christ's day would allow a woman to count coins into his hand, lest he unknowingly be contaminated.[56] Naturally, it is difficult to comprehend how such strict norms could be obliged while crowds of people pushed against one another in the circumstances Mark describes. But if there is merit to these claims, one can imagine the apprehension with which the woman shrank back into the crowd when Jesus asked his pointed question, "Who touched my clothes?"

Jesus' reaction, however, was totally inoffensive. He had felt divine power leave his body the moment the woman touched him, and no doubt knew that someone had been healed, God acting through his person on the basis of some individual's faith. The disciples found his question amusing, in that dozens of people were clamoring about him touching, stroking and bumping him constantly. Yet his question was serious, and he looked around from face to face to determine who had been the recipient of his power. Then, in great fear of reprimand, the woman fell forward at his feet trembling and confessed. She explained the matter, no doubt expecting Jesus to rebuke her and hurry off to a priest to begin his own period of cleansing. But no rebuke followed. Instead, Jesus said: "Daughter, your faith has made you well; go in peace, and be healed of your affliction."

The account reveals several features in the mind of Christ. Primarily it displays the Lord's lack of concern for the manifold ordinances of Judaism by which individuals were thought to be pure or impure religiously. He was the Lord of the Sabbath, and fully comprehended the objectives of the Law of Moses from a divine standpoint. He also comprehended the shallowness of thinking that either food, drink, or physical dirt made one spiritually unclean or that rituals, ablutions and animal sacrifices could cleanse. The thought of being touched by a menstruating woman in no way disturbed Jesus, for he had come to free women from such archaic taboos.

Secondly, Jesus openly declares the availability of his power because of the woman's personal faith. This fact elevates the quality and the value of a woman before God to a level second to no man. Thirdly, Jesus' valediction, "Go in peace, be healed of your affliction," imparts a permanent release from her agitation over a wretched existence, and affirms the unity of the will of Christ with the Father in elevating her situation in daily life.

The Syrophoenician Woman

A few months before his last journey to Jerusalem, Jesus entered upon a new phase of his ministry. In and around the outskirts of Galilee he spent much time teaching about his imminent death and resurrection. During this period he passed through the region of Tyre and Sidon, where he was approached by a certain woman to cast a demon out of her daughter.[57] Matthew refers to the woman as a Canaanite, while Mark says she was a Greek, a Syrophoenician by race. In view of Matthew's intended Jewish audience one can understand why he does not mention, as does Mark, that Jesus entered into a house in this heathen territory, but rather represents the woman as coming out of those boundaries to see him. The reputation of Jesus had preceded him to the district of Tyre and Sidon, and the woman probably had decided already to seek his aid if he ever came her way. She may have been a "God fearer," since a knowledge of Jewish affairs is evidenced by the wording of her urgent plea at Jesus' feet, especially her recognition that he was the Son of David.[58] Her cry, according to Matthew, is met with silence. While Mark records an immediate verbal response to the woman groveling at Jesus' feet in a house, Matthew leaves the impression that Jesus was outside, perhaps on the open road, and continued walking with the woman following behind. Matthew also adds that the disciples requested that Jesus dismiss her fearing that she might create a commotion, for, they said, "She is shouting out after us."

An explanation for his refusal is directed not to the woman but to the disciples, and is harmonious with the emphasis of his mission thus far, to those of the house of Israel only. But the woman's persistent plea and her worship is met with a second refusal which might appear unduly harsh: "It is not good to take the children's bread and throw it to the dogs." Although some scholars understand Jesus' reference to dogs to be a reflection of the typical Jewish attitude toward Gentiles, his rebuff was devoid of contempt. The diminutive *kunaria* does not refer to the ownerless mongrels of the street, but rather to the little pet dogs who played in the house with the children. The Lord's refusal, therefore, merely points out that his blessings, at least in this stage of God's plan, are to be dispensed among Jews alone, and that it would not be appropriate to share them with those Gentiles who dwell among the "children."

The woman's retort reveals a marvelous degree of persistent faith. She not only picks up the Lord's play on the diminutive *kunaria* but adds another, *psichia*, suggesting her humility in being prepared to accept even the "smallest crumbs" that fall from the Master's table. Without objection she consents wholeheartedly to the arrangement of the Messianic mission and restricts her further plea to the figurative language of Jesus, begging, as would a dog beneath the table. Both writers suggest the Lord's delight in the woman's answer and faith by the immediate grant of her request.

As in the case of the woman with an issue of blood, here is displayed the extraordinary power of persistent faith. It is noteworthy that of two recorded cases of Jesus' complimenting the faith of a Gentile, one is a woman,[59] and of seven cases of faith being mentioned as the basis of healing or forgiveness by Christ, three are women.[60]

The Woman with a Crooked Spine

While Jesus was teaching in the synagogue, there appeared a woman who for eighteen years had been bowed together by what Luke describes as "a spirit of infirmity."[61] Geldenhuys speculates that her malady was *spondylitis deformans*, by which "the bones of her spine were fused into a rigid mass."[62] Such was her state that she walked about bent over, completely unable to straighten her back. When Jesus saw her he brought his teaching to a halt and called her to him. He laid his hands on her, saying, "Woman, you are freed from your sickness." The result was an immediate uproar in the synagogue because Jesus had healed on the Sabbath. Jesus retorted:

> You hypocrites, does not each of you on the Sabbath untie his ox or his donkey from the stall, and lead him away to water him? And this woman, a daughter of Abraham as she is, whom Satan has bound for eighteen long years, should she not have been released from this bond on the Sabbath day?

According to Luke, those who had criticized were put to shame, and the crowd rejoiced for the glorious wonders which Jesus did. Nothing else is said of the woman, but the brief account illustrates Jesus' compassion for her condition and his desire to give assistance even when unsolicited. Donald Guthrie expresses the opinion that the incident was recorded primarily to illustrate the weakness of legalism in its approach to human problems:

> Enthusiasm for the Law is admirable, but when religious observance becomes more important than human needs, decay has set in. Jesus did not advocate slavish devotion to legalism. If most Christians had always followed him in this, much of the tragic acrimony in church history would have been avoided. Cherished forms, liturgies and church order need reexamination so that we may discover whether or not, in our enthusiasm to retain them, we are preventing "bent" lives from becoming straightened.[63]

Women Who Gave Money

Several women are worthy of special note because of their recognition, either by Jesus or by Gospel writers, for their contribution of money. In Judaism finances were necessary for the maintenance of the temple and the priests, and for the provision of essentials in regular religious observances. Much the same was and is true of the Christian community, although Jewish laws included compulsory tithes and taxes whereas Christianity was maintained by freewill offerings. It is generally taken for granted that men, who are typically the family heads and principal wage earners, also carry the bulk of religious contribution. It will be shown later, however, that women in the early church had a part in giving, both through financial aid and through charity and hospitality. Likewise, it is noteworthy that in the Gospels the only individuals who are mentioned as providing financial support to Jesus' ministry are women, and the only individual whose contribution to the temple treasury is noted with favor by Jesus is a woman.

Ministering Women. In Luke 8:1–3 special mention is made of three women, among many others, who "contributed to their support out of their private means." Mary Magdalene, to be discussed later, no doubt felt deep appreciation for the exorcism performed upon her by Jesus, for Luke says she had been possessed by seven devils. Joanna was the wife of Chuza, a steward of Herod, and was probably a wealthy and influencial woman. Of Susanna nothing else is known, and the others are unnamed. But Mark 15:40–41 mentions that Mary, the mother of James the Less and Joses, and Salome were also among the great number of women who ministered unto him in Galilee. The entire group must have had money, and considered it a privilege to support Jesus and his disciples on their tours about the country. Likewise, Jesus must have regarded their services to his ministry as honorable and significant in the sight of God.

The Widow's Mite. During the last week of his ministry, probably on Tuesday if the traditional schedule is correct, Jesus sat down to rest in the Court of Women near one of thirteen alms boxes, each designated for a particular purpose.[64] He no doubt was weary from long, contentious discussions with religious leaders. He watched unimpressed as numerous wealthy men cast their gifts into the treasury. Then his attention was seized by a poor widow, perhaps thin and dressed in rags, who dropped two small copper coins into the box. There is evidence that two mites, or *lepta* as they are called here, constituted the smallest acceptable offering of this sort. Jesus somehow realized that the woman had given all that she had. Calling his disciples, he made of her an example stating:

> Truly I say to you, this poor widow put in more than all of them: for they all out of their surplus put into the offering; but she out of her poverty put in all that she had to live on.[65]

Pointing to the wealthy givers who were still in sight and to the gifts already in the boxes, Jesus declared that her gift was the greatest. They had a surplus while she had a deficit. She deserved to receive from them, or from the treasury itself. Yet, out of her deficient store she gave all she had. But what made her gift all the more praiseworthy is that while pledges were exacted from all adult Jewish males, gifts of minors, slaves and women were made by choice. She gave because she wanted to.[66]

Mary Magdalene

The four Gospel writers find it impossible to agree on the details of the crucifixion, burial and resurrection of Christ, but the faithfulness of a large group of women, and the prominence of Mary Magdalene during these events, is attested by all.[67] Only these stayed with Jesus through the crucifixion, and they were the first to see the empty tomb. Daniel-Rops describes this group of faithful women as:

> ... bolder than men, responding more readily to love than to prudence, perhaps better equipped by nature to accept facts beyond the power of reason to analyse, but which their unconscious being could perceive with extraordinary certainty.[68]

Other than his own mother, Mary Magdalene is clearly the most famous woman in the life of Jesus of Nazareth.

A man's interest in a woman can easily become suspect, and criticism of Jesus has been launched on these very grounds. Many critics have suggested that Jesus' relationship with Mary Magdalene was intimate, but secretive so as not to mar his reputation of sinlessness. Yet in defense of Christ's purity, Daniel-Rops says that his heart "was a crystal without a flaw."

Mary clearly receives her name from the town of Magdala, in the province of Galilee. Her appearance prior to the Passion Narrative is confined to Luke 8:2, where she is listed among the ministering women and identified as the one "from whom seven demons had gone out." She is not to be identified with "the sinful woman" who anoints Jesus in Galilee, for the Lukan narrative introduces her afresh in chapter eight, in no way connecting her to the incident at Simon's house recorded in the previous chapter. Nor can the claim be made that she was a psychotic, given to hallucinations as a result of the extreme malady from which Jesus had cured her. These, and other allegations, have been made to discredit her report of the resurrection, and are met with disapproval by scholars in general.

Mary appears at the crucifixion in the company of several women who had journeyed with Jesus from Galilee, including Jesus' mother. She is also present at the burial of Jesus, and from the Lukan account it can be inferred that she observed closely where the body was laid, intending to return after the Sabbath to further dress it with spices and ointments. But of special significance is Mary's prominence in the Johannine record of the resurrection.

A number of details in the four Gospels concerning the resurrection simply cannot be harmonized: the number of angels, one or two; whether Mary Magdalene arrived alone, or in the company of several women; whether it was still dark, twilight or at the rising of the sun; whether the angels appeared before or after Peter and John made their visit to the tomb; and whether Jesus appeared to the group of women or to Mary Magdalene only. But Mark 16:9 clearly states that Jesus appeared first to Mary Magdalene, and this testimony supports the detailed account in the Fourth Gospel.[69]

The Evangelist does not give an explanation for Mary remaining outside the sepulchre weeping after everyone else had left the garden. But her solitude and her repeated investigation in search of the missing precious body clearly give rise to the appearance of two heavenly messengers. The plural *oidamen* in Mary's reply suggests that she was not alone, no doubt still accompanied by the women mentioned by the Synoptists. But the writer is brief at this point, apparently anxious to describe the subsequent visit of Peter and the beloved disciple. The figure whom Mary mistakes for the gardener asks her the same question as did the angels, and her response indicates no suspicion of Jesus' resurrection.

The difficulty in recognizing Jesus arises from two causes. First, there was a change in the external appearance of Jesus, which amounted to "another form." In seeing him again even those who knew him well required time and also the observation of simple mannerisms by which his identity might be disclosed. Second, the grotesque vividness of his death shortly before had devastated any mental or emotional expectation of seeing him alive.

A highlight of the pericope is the tone with which the name of Mary comes from Jesus' lips, to awaken her faith and cause her very soul to quiver. Some see in this a literary device to illuminate the parable of the Good Shepherd, in which the disciples of Jesus are compared to sheep who know their Master's voice when he calls them by name. Having turned her face to the grave before he spoke, Mary turned sharply at the sound of his voice, and put all her being into the cry *rabboni*, meaning "my teacher" or "my master," a term of great respect.

Jesus' foreboding statement "touch me not . . ." is troublesome. Forbidding Mary to touch his body seems completely incompatible with the invitation which he later gives to Thomas to examine his wounds. Furthermore, reason offers no explanation as to why a human touch would in any way violate the being of him who had conquered all. Rather, it is likely that Jesus was telling Mary that she should not cling to him as if he had returned to restore old relationships. His earthly mission was accomplished, he had returned to evidence his victory, and then to say goodbye.

There is a clear mission quality in the testimony of Mary to the other disciples. Especially noteworthy is the fact that she, not Peter, was the first to see the risen Jesus. No doubt for this reason in some Gnostic quarters Mary Magdalene, rather than Peter, became the most prominent witness to the teaching of the risen Lord, and in the western church she became known as "the apostle to the apostles."

Glimpses into the mind of Jesus obtainable from Gospel traditions make it quite clear that women held a position of striking significance in his life and ministry. Although he seems to have played down any prominence achieved by his own mother, lest such should detract from the greater importance of his own ministry, he treated her with utmost tenderness and respect. The Gospel records, especially Luke and John, give special attention to women as objects of Jesus' concern for socially undesirable classes, and vividly portray his compassion for their plight. His conversation with the Samaritan woman, and his physical contact with the woman suffering an issue of blood, illustrate Jesus' disregard for traditional taboos and purity laws where individuals are concerned. His praise for Mary of Bethany, and contrasting rebuke for Martha, establish the right of women to set aside domestic chores in favor of spiritual pursuits. The pardon extended to the woman taken in adultery and the sinful woman who anointed his feet are indicative of Jesus' compassionate concern for lives marred by sin, and his acknowledgment of penitence even from individuals least acceptable in religious circles. The story of the Syrophoenician woman portrays the great potential of a woman's persistent plea for divine favor, as well as offering a preview of Jesus' universal mission. His commendation for the widow and for various ministering women stresses the acceptability of financial aid which women might offer for a noble cause. And the stories of the Samaritan woman and Mary Magdalene strongly suggest the potential in women as agents of evangelism.

In all, the attitude of Christ towards women elucidates the revolutionary nature of his ministry, and provides the principles upon which their dignity and equity might be promoted in the early Christian community.

III. MARRIAGE AND DIVORCE

Marcello Craveri suggests that the Christian concept of marriage was neither a new idea nor an old one revised, but arose progressively "by crossbreeding the Hebraic institution with the Roman."[70] Certainly, one can recognize a number of features of the Christian view of marriage well established in Roman society before the time of Christ. For example, the Roman matron occupied a considerably more noble status than wives of contemporary cultures, and the Roman view of marriage as a "guardianship" suggested that women should be protected, because of a weaker nature, rather than owned as if occupying an inferior status. Roman society upheld monogamous marriage based on love and fidelity, and the Roman wife had equal rights of inheritance. Even the English word "matrimony" is derived from the Latin *matris munia*, meaning "duties of the mother." Furthermore, if a husband committed adultery his wife had the right to sue for divorce.

However, the qualities of the marriage institution in Roman society are easily exaggerated. Numerous classical writers complained of prolific divorce and the decay of the home resulting from infidelity and disrespect for marriage by Romans in general. The ease with which Romans could obtain divorces, allowing women also to divorce their husbands for virtually any cause, can hardly be considered more noble than the Jewish system.

What is more significant than either the shortcomings or the qualities of Jewish and Roman concepts of marriage is the fact that Christian marriage did not simply evolve out of other societies, but rather sprang from the revolutionary mind of Jesus Christ. It is essential to recognize that Jesus' teachings and attitudes served as a foundation upon which was constructed the doctrine and practice of the early Christian community, and relatively speaking bridged the gap between Judaism and Christianity, and between

Old and New Testaments. Therefore, it is essential that the basis for a response of the New Testament to the status of women in antiquity would lie in Christ's own teaching, and this is especially true concerning marriage and divorce.

Controversy Among Jesus' Contemporaries

Jesus' teaching concerning both marriage and divorce must be viewed in terms of the assumption by his contemporaries that divorce could be taken for granted.[71] Apparently for centuries there had existed a very callous attitude among Jewish males toward their wives, suitably illustrated by the advice of Jesus ben Sirach: "If she go not as you would have her go, cut her off and give her a bill of divorce."[72]

Closer to the time of Christ, contentions developed among rabbis concerning the grounds for divorce, and in particular the meaning of "some indecency" in Deuteronomy 24:1ff. The dominant school of Hillel understood the law as permitting divorce for anything which might be displeasing to the husband, even the innocent error of burning food. The more conservative followers of R. Shammai understood "some indecency" to mean adultery, or anything which constituted justifiable grounds for the accusation of adultery. A century later, the school of R. Akiba allowed divorce simply if the husband found a more desirable wife.

As the fame of Jesus spread as a great teacher and prophet, one would expect that at least on one occasion his opinion on this controversial issue would be sought by Jewish leaders, and it is in such a context that two of the four relevant discourses are found.[73]

A question arises concerning possible sinister motives on the part of the Pharisees to whom both the Matthaean and Markan accounts attribute questions about divorce. Attempts to test Jesus were characteristic of the Pharisees and Sadducees, and represent their desire either to ensnare him in words and technicalities, or perhaps even to find cause for accusing him of blasphemy. But in Matthew 19 the only apparent reason for questioning Jesus was to determine whether he would side with the school of Hillel or with the more conservative school of Shammai, for the question presupposes an acceptance of divorce and is merely concerned with the grounds, that is, whether divorce could be granted for "every cause." No doubt the question, as here intended, could have been put to Jesus, "What did Moses mean by the expression 'some indecency'?" Mark's version of the incident has the group asking simply whether it is lawful for a man to divorce his wife, which appears not to be concerned with the controversy between rabbinical schools but an attempt to draw Jesus into contradicting the Law of Moses.

It is important to note the object of divorce and the purpose of a bill of divorcement in the minds of Jesus' contemporaries. It is almost axiomatic that a man who put away his wife did so in order to marry another, or to freely look for another to marry. It mattered little whether his excuse was adultery, poor cooking, failing beauty, barrenness or intolerable mannerisms. The Jew who sought to divorce his wife had in mind taking another wife when he became free from the first one. This is even implied in Jesus' postulate "whoever divorces his wife and marries another." Once a husband determined to do so, if he could find any fault which could be construed as suitable grounds according to the current interpretation of the Law of Moses, all he had to do was to repudiate her. There was no legal procedure, nor was her consent necessary.

But it was also assumed that the repudiated wife would desire remarriage, and to afford that privilege a bill of divorcement was placed in her hand upon sending her out of the house. The Mosaic provision for divorce seems not so much directed at the morality of physical relationships as for the provision of some protection of a woman from multiple claims of conjugal rights. The bill of divorcement was a certificate to which a repudiated wife was entitled, whereby she could prove her freedom to remarry and guarantee any man with whom she might cohabit that he was not violating the rights of another man. Therefore, the bill of divorcement should not be thought of as a legal certificate of divorce — that is, the writ by which a legal marriage was dissolved — but written evidence of what had already taken place. Josephus describes the object of the procedure according to Hillel:

> He that desires to be divorced from his wife for any cause whatsoever (and many such causes happen among men) let him in writing give assurance that he will never use her as his wife anymore, for by these means she may be at liberty to marry another husband, although before this bill of deliverance be given she is not permitted to do so.[74]

At first the bill of divorcement was very simple, reading something like: "Let this be from me your writ of divorce and deed of liberation, that you may marry whatsoever man you will." As time went on the writ became longer, and more technically involved.

Jesus' View of Marriage

Christianity brought about significant changes in world attitudes toward marriage, primarily through religious sentiments, such as reverence for the commandments of God and fear of punishment for evil, which in turn led to higher morals and penitential discipline. The root of this positive trend, and the basis of the Christian doctrine of marriage, was the teaching of Christ that from creation God's intended pattern for marriage was the union of one man and one woman for life. Bornkamm writes that Jesus' respect for marriage is one of the clearest departures from Jewish tradition, and a principal reason for rejecting any attempt to connect him with any ascetic group such as the Essenes.[75] Although Jesus never married, his teachings give no indication that his celibate life was one of religious conviction. It appears rather that the intense nature of his mission, the implications of his divine incarnation, problems which might have arisen among his followers had he left physical descendants and perhaps numerous other factors were at the root of his voluntary celibacy. Jesus was totally committed to a task which allowed for no mundane demands such as those essential in marriage.

Although Jesus remained single as a personal expedient, he had the utmost respect for marriage. His presence at the wedding feast in Cana is at least some indication of his approval of marriage as an institution. But of extreme importance is a statement uttered in opposition to divorce, preserved in slightly different forms in both Matthew and Mark:

> He who created them from the beginning made them male and female, and said, For this cause a man shall leave his father and mother, and shall cleave to his wife; and the two shall become one flesh. Consequently they are no longer two, but one flesh. What therefore God has joined together, let no man separate.[76]

This statement represents the extent of our knowledge of Christ's teaching on marriage, save the related material on divorce which actually provides the context for the above statement. Yet a great deal is implied in the single utterance. It is clear that to Jesus marriage was a divine institution, established at the beginning of man's history. As to whether monogamy is traceable to the earliest societies there is still considerable debate. But countless notable biblical scholars see Jesus as here confirming the monogamous marriage system as God intended it from the creation. The almost poetic description of the blending of male and female into one flesh is taken from the creation narrative, and reflects an early traditional requirement that a new couple leave parental homes and establish a household of their own. Jesus uses the quotation to emphasize that a marriage is not simply an agreement between a male and a female which may be dissolved verbally, nor merely a legal contract which may be dissolved by civil procedures, but rather a physical, mental and spiritual "yoking" of two people in the mind of God. When two people marry, their relationship is regarded as a matrimonial bond because "God has joined" them together.

Concerning this divine design it appears that the strong cohesive force of sex was purposed by God to be at least one factor suggesting an inseparable unity. The use of the Greek terms *arsen* and *thule* together suggests that Jesus understood the purpose of the sexes to be fulfilled in marriage. Therefore, since marriage bonds are registered and validated by God, Jesus says that it is not the place of man to assume the authority of dissolving them.

Some commentators understand the prohibition "let no man separate" to refer to the husband, as opposed to judicial authority, since in Jewish custom the husband alone would be the instigator of divorce proceedings. But the shift of terms from *arsen* to *anthropos* suggests that Jesus had in mind neither the will of the husband nor a judicial authority, but the whims of humanity in general. A relationship such as marriage, which has divine approval, should not be profaned by divorce.

Markan Priority

Having taken note of Jesus' high regard for marriage, the next step is to give consideration to the obvious tension existing within the longer Matthaean divorce passage, and between Matthew and the other two Synoptics. Within Matthew alone there is sufficient disharmony to suspect that either the writer or a later editor has woven together different divorce sayings and presented them in the form of controversy dialogues. Furthermore, it seems that in Matthew certain statements are imputed to Jesus which he could not have made in light of his teaching on marriage.

Of the four divorce sections in the Synoptics, only Matthew includes a question about divorce "for every cause" and Jesus' alleged concession on grounds of unchastity. If Jesus actually made a concession in agreement with Shammai, as suggested by Matthew 19, his position in verse 8 of that chapter where he relativizes Deuteronomy 24:1 is conspicuously out of place. Verses 4–7 naturally lead up to verse 8, and comprise a sensible unit. But this section does not discuss grounds for divorce and is in fact awkward following the question in verse 3, which it reputedly answers. Moreover, verse 9, which includes the "except for fornication" concession, fails to follow the previous five verses naturally and smoothly, and represents an obvious lapse in logic on the part of the writer. It appears then that verse 9 replaced another ending to verses 4–8, and is inserted here to present Jesus as siding with Shammai against the school of Hillel.

There are some who insist that the Matthaean form of the divorce material is the original, with the Markan and Lukan forms representing accommodations to Roman and Hellenistic readers. But it is abundantly clear that the Markan form, along with Q, was used by the author of Matthew to construct a rendition of Jesus' teaching on marriage and divorce more acceptable to a Jewish audience, and to present him as holding the most conservative rabbinic view.[77] When all the secondary elements are removed from Matthew the resultant form is amazingly similar to Mark, and it must be admitted that Matthew is inclined to assimilate to rabbinic patterns. But whereas some feel that the exception was added by a Jewish Christian who "rabbinized" Christ's sayings, there is greater reason to think that the addition was made by the author himself.

The fact that neither Mark, Luke nor Paul displays any knowledge of a concession on grounds of unchastity is further evidence that Jesus did not actually argue in the manner presented in Matthew. To the contrary, Jesus' own teaching indicates his conviction concerning the permanent nature of the matrimonial bond, and one might infer from his general teaching on forgiveness that infidelity should never be cause for repudiation by one's partner. It is simply unlike Jesus to make that kind of exception.

Markan priority must also be seen in the disharmony between Matthew 19 and Mark 10, concerning whether divorce was a Mosaic command or a concession. Matthew has the Pharisees asking Jesus why Moses commanded (*eneteilato*) men to give a bill of divorcement and to divorce (*apolusai*) their wives, to which Jesus responds that Moses permitted (*epetrepsen*) such action because of the hardness of their hearts. Mark records a rhetorical question from Jesus, "What did Moses command?" with a reply from the Pharisees, "Moses allowed . . . ." To this Jesus replies, "for the hardness of your hearts he wrote you this precept" (*entole*). Some see the verbs "to command" and "to permit" as equally appropriate in this context, since Deuteronomy 24:1-4 involves specific requirements under contingent circumstances and occurs in a larger section containing "commands."

Note must be taken, however, of the fact that Deuteronomy does not command the repudiation of an unfaithful wife, but rather commands giving a bill of divorce to such a repudiated wife. The practice of divorce is presupposed. Furthermore, both grammatically and contextually the treatment of divorce itself in Deuteronomy 24:1ff must be taken as a license rather than a command, and it is certain that Jewish scholars of Jesus' day knew this to be so. Therefore, the Markan form of the question and answer between Jesus and the Pharisees is perfectly sensible. Had the law commanded divorce, there would be no point in asking Jesus if the practice was lawful. However, certain rabbinic schools taught that divorcing an unfaithful wife was a duty, and it is certain that Matthew reversed the terms "command" and "permit" to accentuate this notion. But it is precisely here that the Matthaean account becomes awkward, since neither the Pharisaic suggestion of a command, nor Jesus' suggestion of a concession, is compatible with the original question, "Is it lawful . . . for every cause?" Therefore, the form of this statement as it appears in Mark is clearly closer to Jesus' original words.

For the benefit of readers coming from a more conservative or fundamentalist background, these considerations may appear somewhat radical. But exact scholarship must consider all factual evidence and cannot ignore certain inescapable truths surrounding the origin and transmission of biblical texts.

Jesus Rejects Moses

Two statements made by Jesus suggest that he rejected the Law of Moses as far as divorce is concerned. The first is that Moses permitted divorce "because of the hardness of your hearts," and the second is the declaration that "from the beginning it was not so," found only in Matthew but perfectly in keeping with the sense of Mark 10:6. The intervention of sin has worked havoc in marriages, and some provision for dissolving the matrimonial bond has entered virtually every society because of the inclinations of human beings. But according to Jesus this was contrary to the will of God from the beginning of time.

For this reason he began his reply with an appeal to the pattern set for marriage in creation. On this basis he established that marriage is a holy institution taken too lightly by his contemporaries, and by most societies before his time, and that the Mosaic provision for divorce was not intended to condone or to sanction husbands putting away their wives, but to limit sinfulness and to place some control upon its consequences. Jesus, therefore, in no way confirmed the Mosaic concession, but to the contrary denounced it by pointing out the degenerate nature of a society which openly sanctions the dissolution of marriages which God holds sacred. From the ideal standpoint, says Jesus, marriage is indissoluble and requires a lifetime of unbroken mutual love and faithfulness with no room for divorce.

In addition to his appeal to created order, Jesus drew attention to the natural consequences of divorce as justification for denouncing the Mosaic concession, and in so doing found it necessary to redefine the concept of adultery (*moicheia*). According to rabbinical law a husband could not commit adultery against his wife, for adultery was understood to be "intercourse between a married woman and a man other than her husband." But according to Jesus, when a man puts away his wife regardless of the reason and marries another, his taking a second wife is to be considered adultery because God recognizes his former marriage as still binding. Likewise, the repudiated wife, if she marries, becomes an adulteress. Although the bill of divorce according to tradition declared her free to marry, God regards her as the wife of her first husband. Furthermore, the man who marries the "put away" wife commits adultery by taking another man's wife.

In spite of the divine nature of a marital union, there is little reason to think it deeply immoral for a husband and wife who find their relationship unbearable to part and go their separate ways. The apostle Paul suggests that such might become necessary under certain circumstances. But the complication which renders divorce unacceptable before God, so Jesus implies, is that the parties involved invariably remarry when free from their former partners. When they do so, Jesus says, they commit adultery.

A Higher Estimate of the Status of Women

The impact of Christ's teaching must have been staggering to his contemporaries. The rabbis recognized that if a wife had relations with another man, the two parties committed adultery against the husband. But her actions were never considered a violation of her first marriage if her husband had divorced her. Even further from their thinking was the notion that a man could commit adultery against his former wife. This teaching was certainly revolutionary, and without a doubt represents an effort on the part of Jesus to elevate the status of women.

Redefining adultery involves a higher estimate of the status of women than was current in the contemporary society of Jesus. The prevalence of divorce among Jews was clearly linked with the inferior status of women and with the fact that relevant scriptures had been interpreted and rabbinical laws enacted in ways which were grossly slanted in favor of male interests.

It is on this point precisely that some scholars call in question the Markan form of the divorce material. Since Jewish law did not allow a woman to divorce her husband, it is argued that Jesus could not have implied that possibility, as Mark 10:12 suggests, particularly in a discourse with Pharisees. If this contention is valid, one is forced to regard the Markan record at this point to be an accommodation of Jesus' actual words to a Roman audience, perhaps extricating the possibility of Matthaean priority.

But even at this place Mark displays greater historical accuracy than does Matthew. The original discourse certainly sprang from rabbinical inquiries, but Jesus' treatment of marriage and divorce resorted to pre–Israelite principles and implied universal application. This alone suggests Jesus' concern for divorce problems outside Palestine and his possible familiarity with the right of western women to sue for divorce. If so, he worded his statement to cover all customs. But it is even more likely that Jesus would direct himself to a principle which had been violated in certain notorious instances in Palestine. According to Josephus, this was precisely the sin of Herodias, who was rebuked by John the Baptist for her marriage to Herod Antipas, and later the action of Salome to her husband Costobarus in direct violation of Jewish law.[78] Mark stands alone in this implication, however, for only the conduct of males is called in question by the writer of Matthew 19 and the source common to Matthew and Luke.

Jesus, therefore, represents an elevated view of the role of women in his teaching on divorce, in that he offers a higher degree of protection from repudiation than did the Law of Moses. But perhaps more important is his implication that women have a responsibility equal to that of husbands to uphold the divine pattern for marriage, and to avoid adulterous relationships such as those condoned for centuries by the concession of the Law.[79]

Hermeneutical Difficulties

Interpretation of the Synoptic divorce material is made difficult by the presence of "except for fornication" in Matthew, and it is concerning this alleged concession that most ecclesiastical debate has arisen. The subject cannot be concluded without at least a brief mention of the complications which arise if one accepts the phrase as originating with Jesus. While it is doubtful that Jesus actually made this concession, there is little question concerning its presence in the earliest manuscripts of Matthew. Therefore, it would appear that the liberty of modifying Jesus' words in order to accommodate a conservative Jewish audience must have been taken by the original writer, or an editor prior to the oldest extant copies.

The term *porneia*, meaning "harlotry" or "fornication," is generally regarded as any illicit sexual behavior which might be considered as a violation of marital fidelity. The writer probably selected this term for the concession to avoid confusion with *moicheia*, and to comply with the "unchastity" of Deuteronomy 24:1–2. It is impossible to know whether the term suggests a single act, or whether it must be an established lifestyle of illicit sexual behavior.

The implication of Shammai's interpretation of Deuteronomy 24:1–2 is that regardless of the basically indissoluble nature of marriage from the standpoint of God, if a partner is unfaithful to the vows of marital fidelity by engaging in sexual relations with another party, the wronged party is justified in choosing to dissolve the marriage. More important, if Jesus sided with this view his implication was that under exceptional circumstances God will comply with the wishes of the injured party by permitting freedom from his (or her) unfaithful partner. This possibility has Jesus offering a tolerance of divorce when a marriage partner has become guilty of fornication, and in such cases the choice of maintaining or dissolving the marriage lies with the injured party.

On the basis of the spurious concession, some scholars have concluded that the act of fornication itself brings about an automatic dissolution of the marital bond. If such were the case, the implication is that a secret commission of adultery by one partner would automatically change their marriage into fornication, since they would no longer be husband and wife. The innocent party in this case, against whom the secret adultery had been committed, would unknowingly become a partner in an immoral relationship thinking the marriage to be perfectly sound. Such a suggestion is unthinkable.

A further interpretive difficulty concerns the right of remarriage. From the birth of the church to modern times there has been constant dispute as to whether Jesus extended the right of remarriage to divorced persons. In the post-apostolic era Clement of Alexandria, Origen, Chrysostom, Tertullian, Jerome and others accepted divorce provided the wife was at fault, upholding the age-old tolerance of extramarital relations by husbands, but they allowed no remarriage to divorcees. Augustine was a bit more lenient, allowing husbands to divorce wives for barrenness, and permitting the husbands to remarry, but not repudiated wives. Later the Roman Catholic Church came to accept divorce only in the case of fornication, but denied the right of remarriage even to the innocent party. Most Protestant groups have upheld the Catholic toleration of divorce for adultery, although allowing remarriage to the innocent party only. In cases where parties have divorced for trivial causes neither party is granted the right of remarriage, considering that any such marriage would constitute adultery in the sight of God. Still others have suggested that the right of divorce and remarriage is tolerated by God among non-believers, much after the fashion of the Mosaic concession, but among Christians he allows neither.

It should be kept in mind that the right of remarriage is extended only by vague implication in those places in Matthew where "except for fornication" appears, and the historicity of this concession has been called in question already. If the words were genuinely uttered by Jesus, the subject of remarriage would still be difficult to resolve since nothing further is said about it by New Testament writers. But the most logical interpretation of the entire body of divorce material, if the concession is included, is that when a husband or wife divorces a partner for fornication the marriage is then dissolved completely in the mind of God, and both parties have the right of remarriage regardless of wrongs committed. In spite of the appearance that a wife might reap the benefits of infidelity by being freed religiously to marry whom she chooses, this theory is still the most acceptable. There is no suggestion in the Synoptics that an individual who is divorced for infidelity must pay a penalty for his sin by living the rest of his days in penitential celibacy. Nor is it reasonable to think that a man or woman would be bound perpetually to a marriage which has been dissolved, or that adultery can be committed against a marriage which no longer exists.

Many conservative churches today struggle with the implications of

Jesus' statements on divorce and remarriage. Feeling compelled both to regulate the behavior of their members and to control entrance to the kingdom of God, they are inclined to extract more from these passages than is actually there. For example, following Catholic tradition some declare second marriages (without valid cause for divorce) to be "a state of continuous adultery" and refuse church membership until and unless the immoral marriage is dissolved. Church members who do such are permanently disfellowshipped.

The rules of Greek grammar are often oversimplified and exploited to facilitate doctrinal apologetics. In this case the use of the present tense of *moicheuein* does not convey the notion that one who remarries after an unexcused divorce "goes on committing adultery," or that such a marriage constitutes a "state of continuous adultery." Nor is there sound biblical basis for withholding the right of remarriage to divorced persons.

The point of Jesus' teaching was to expose the hypocrisy in using the technicalities of the Law of Moses for personal benefit. Neither Jesus nor later New Testament writers set down any rules for unraveling complex marital relationships, nor do they suggest or offer any basis for withholding God's grace and church fellowship from converts, pending evidence of penitence and due restitution.

Such ecclesiastical dogma arises from the human desire for technical clarity and from the degenerate inclination to control and manipulate each other. The very nature of such regulations is void of the spirit of God.

The ministry of Jesus was highly instrumental in elevating the status of women. His approach to marriage and divorce, in particular, set a higher moral standard for all classes and societies, and thereby provided a higher degree of protection for women against the evil tendencies of human vice, as well as a higher degree of responsibility for wives in the maintenance of successful and godly marriages.

The teachings of Jesus in general brought together the more noble principles of all societies before his time, and likewise pointed out numerous shortcomings of social and religious standards. But his doctrines were neither borrowed from society nor acquired from religious sects. Instead they should be regarded by the Christian church as divinely inspired in response to degenerate norms of the ancient world, and with a view to establishing the foundation principles of the kingdom of God. For Christians, his mind, attitudes and actions represent the ultimate revelation of divine will for humanity. Therefore, concerning the status of women in the Christian community, Jesus is the key.

2. Prominent Women in Various Apostolic Churches

With the establishment of the New Testament church, certain changes became visible among the disciples of Christ in their attitude toward the status of women. No doubt such changes represented the practical application of the revolutionary teachings of Jesus concerning social injustice and religious hypocrisy. But the results were far-reaching and became especially evident in the writings of Paul and in the Lukan record of Paul's ministry. The most obvious factor in this regard is that women were subject to the same personal response to the Gospel message as men. Beginning with the sermon of Peter on Pentecost, women were called to repentance, faith and confession of Christ without discrimination. They were subjected to immersion, named among the believers and encouraged to participate in various acts of godly service in the daily activities of the Christian community. As churches were established in Palestine, Asia Minor and Europe, women not only found meaningful roles but also attained prominence and notoriety.

I. JERUSALEM

During the early stages of the church the apostles so dominate the historical picture that little treatment is given by Luke to the activities of converts individually, whether men or women. The narrative does, however, give sufficient detail so as to reveal the presence of, and significant role of, women in the events surrounding the establishment of the church. Luke retraces the ascension details, adding, for the benefit of transition, an abridged form of Jesus' discourse on the kingdom and Holy Spirit. The writer names the eleven who returned to Jerusalem from the Mount of Ascension to wait for the impending immersion with the Holy Spirit and power foretold by Jesus. Then particular mention is made of certain

41

women, including Mary the mother of Jesus, among approximately one hundred twenty disciples abiding at Jerusalem.[1] Luke's mention of this group of women is perfectly in keeping with their prominence in the Gospels. The group likely includes those who accompanied Jesus from Galilee and those present at the cross and at the grave. Also among this group the mother of Jesus makes her last appearance in the New Testament record. Although no mention is made of any special honor these women might have received, it is clear that they were a recognized part of the larger group from which Matthias was chosen to replace Judas, and that they witnessed the miraculous activities on Pentecost which gave birth to the church.

On that occasion, as a result of the outpouring of the Holy Spirit and the preaching of Peter, three thousand became adherents to the Christian religion. This multitude comprised the Jerusalem church and doubtless included many women. Luke later mentions that the body had grown so that the men alone numbered five thousand.[2]

The first woman among the Jerusalem Christians to be discussed in detail is Sapphira, wife of one Ananias. The story of this couple is one of two examples given by Luke to illustrate the practical results, both positive and negative, of the community of goods operative in the early Jerusalem church.[3] Much of the community consisted of Jews of the Diaspora, having journeyed to Jerusalem for the festive season and having little or no means of support for a long period of time. Apparently, each local Christian who so desired sold possessions and deposited the money with the Apostles for a common fund. Ananias and Sapphira conspired to sell a parcel of land, and give a portion of the income under the pretense of giving all. Their deceit, having become known to the Apostles, was considered a "lie to the Holy Spirit," and "to God." The couple dropped dead in turn, implying a divine execution, and were carried out and buried. The example brought great fear upon the community and the subsequent "signs and wonders" worked by the Apostles resulted in even more conversions, described by Luke as "multitudes of both men and women."

The most prominent woman in the Jerusalem church was Mary, mother of John Mark, and identified by Luke as the sister of Barnabas. There is only one reference to her in scripture, but this mention is significant.[4] The authority for this material, no doubt, is Mark, the son of the household and later author of one of the Gospels. The fact that Peter went to her house directly upon his escape from prison, and that a sizable group had assembled there, suggests that her home was well known by the Jerusalem Christians. It further suggests that her house was of above-average size, and therefore that she was somewhat wealthy. The whole picture of Mary is one of devotion to Christian service and prominence in the Christian community.[5]

II. JOPPA

The Gospel continued to spread from Jerusalem into all Judea and Samaria. Philip the evangelist was the instrument by which salvation came to "both men and women" in the city of Samaria, capital of the district through which Jesus passed when he encountered the woman at the well. Luke gives no record of the establishment of the church in Damascus, but Saul of Tarsus went there with letters from the high priest to arrest Christians, "whether men or women," and conduct them to Jerusalem for trial.[6]

During this period Peter seems to have been the principal instrument in evangelizing the Phoenician coast, for it is he who visited the disciples at Lydda and Joppa.

In Joppa there lived a Christian woman named Dorcas who became ill and died while Peter was in Lydda. Her name is given by the writer as Tabitha in Aramaic, translated into Greek as Dorcas, meaning "gazelle." Luke calls her a disciple (*mathetria*), the only place in the New Testament where the feminine form is used, and describes her as having been "full of good works and almsdeeds." Although the grief expressed by her friends is not unusual in terms of customary mourning rituals, there is every reason to believe that this woman was special. The charity for which the widows of Joppa best remembered her was making garments for the poor. Having been sent for by the disciples at Joppa, the writer says, Peter came down and restored her life by supernatural power.[7] We have no idea how long she may have lived after this event.

The good works of Dorcas live on after her as a testimonial, exemplifying the use of charitable talents in the service of Christ. In modern times many "Dorcas Societies" perpetuate her memory, and in the city of Jaffa there is a memorial in the "Tabitha School" devoted to the care and education of underprivileged girls.[8]

III. LYSTRA

After the conversion of Saul of Tarsus and his subsequent introduction to the church through Barnabas, Luke recounts his commission by the church at Antioch and his first missionary journey. There is no mention of any female converts during the first excursion through Southern Galatia, but on his second visit to Lystra Paul finds the mother of Timothy, "a Jewess who believed."[9] Presumably both Eunice and her son were converted during or subsequent to Paul's first visit to Lystra. To many scholars the verb tense used here indicates that the father of Timothy was deceased, making Eunice a widow.

The name Eunice, meaning "conquering well," is Greek, and her husband was Greek, for which cause Timothy had not been circumcised in childhood. Such a marriage is a reflection of the less exclusive standard of Phrygian Jews than those living in Palestine. But the mother and grand-mother did all in their power to train Timothy in the fear of God and in the knowledge of holy scripture, and for this they are commended by Paul when he later reminds the young evangelist of the unfeigned faith of his mother and grandmother.[10] Apparently Eunice had chosen Timothy's name, rather than his father, since its meaning is "one who honors God," further indicating a desire to rear her son according to Jewish tradition. But having now turned to Christianity, her zeal, and that of the grandmother Lois, is all the stronger.

It is widely thought that the home of Eunice was a center of hospitality for Paul and other traveling evangelists who passed through Lycaonia. Therefore, it is reasonable to conclude that both Eunice and Lois occupied a place of considerable prominence in the early church at Lystra.

IV. PHILIPPI

Philippi was the first prominent city of Macedonia evangelized by the Apostle Paul. Relevant classical writers suggest that the heritage of Macedonian women included considerably greater social freedom than did that of their sisters in Achaia. And in harmony with that impression, the Lukan narrative reveals a much higher degree of self-assertion among Macedonian women in response to Christianity, beginning at Philippi.

Prompted to sail to Macedonia by a heavenly vision, Paul and his company entered the Roman colony Philippi, the capital of Macedonia.[11] After several days they made contact with a group of women who had gathered for prayer on the banks of the river. Among them was a merchant woman of the Lydian city of Thyatira. The name Lydia by which she is identified is probably derived from her home country. Purple dyeing was a flourishing industry in Lydia as early as Homer.[12] There was a guild of dyers there, and this woman had apparently settled along the trade route as a seller of Lydian fabrics. The country of Lydia was itself originally a Macedonian colony, which gives this woman a certain affinity with the heritage of women in Philippi. She is generally thought to have been a widow and wealthy, although her racial name suggests rather a slave class. She therefore may have been a freedwoman. Luke further identifies her as "a God-fearer," or "one that worshipped God." This appellation was applied by Jews to those Gentiles who adhered to the synagogue but had not ac-cepted Judaism to the extent of proselytizing.

The apostles sat down and spoke to the women, and Lydia was quietly attentive, especially to the words of Paul. Luke metaphorically states that the Lord opened her heart to the message and she submitted to baptism. Accompanying her in this act of commitment were all those of her household, a group which may well have included her servants and hired workers, and perhaps also Euodia and Syntyche of Philippians 4:2–3.

After her conversion Lydia opened her home to Paul and his companions. Upon their miraculous release from prison, Paul and Silas returned to her house to exhort the believers before departing to Thessalonica. This leaves the impression that the home of Lydia became the meeting place for the church, at least while it was small in that locality.

The absence of Lydia's name in subsequent New Testament writings has led to much speculation about her identity. Some have suggested that her true name was either Euodia or Syntyche. As early as Clement of Alexandria the conjecture was offered that "the true yokefellow" of Philippians 4:3 was Paul's wife, and none other than Lydia, a rather far-fetched view considering Paul's own claims of celibacy.

Assuming that neither Euodia nor Syntyche can be identified with Lydia, converted perhaps ten years earlier, Paul's reference to them in his letter to the Philippians is noteworthy. These two names were very common in Paul's day, but were worn by two women in particular in the church at Philippi who had labored with him in the Gospel. Paul' words imply their involvement in proclaiming the Gospel in face of great personal danger and opposition, which is indeed a heroic and significant role for women at this stage in history. Chrysostom regarded the pair to be "the chief of the church which was there (at Philippi)."[13] But their mention, clearly of minor and incidental nature, was more of Paul's personal interest than of doctrinal significance to the entire church, and it seems that too much is drawn by some writers from this single brief reference. All we know with certainty about these two women is contained in the relative clause in verse 3, and it is senseless to speculate further.

It cannot be denied, however, that women played a prominent role in the church at Philippi. Of the five named Christians there, three are women. Truly in the conversion of Lydia and the others of interest here a new era had dawned for Europe and for women. Although some deny that Macedonia deserves special credit with regard to the prominence of women, the ancient heritage of feminine liberty in that area is readily visible in this phase of church history.

V. THESSALONICA

After departing from Philippi, Paul's company passed through Amphipolis and Apollonia, and came to Thessalonica.[14] This Macedonian city, situated at the northeast corner of the Thermaic Gulf, was rebuilt in

315 B.C. by Cassander and named after his wife. Since its surrender to the Romans in 168 B.C. the city had been a government seat and headquarters of the proconsul, and since the time of Octavius, around 42 B.C., was a free city. A chief station on the Via Egnatia, Thessalonica must have held great excitement for the evangelists on their first visit.

The company spent three weeks reasoning out of the scriptures with the locals, resulting in the conversion "of the devout Greeks a great multitude, and of the chief women not a few." There is much disagreement among scholars as to the meaning of "chief women." The text reads *gunaikon te ton proton,* which might be understood as "wives of the leading men." The Western editors probably so understood it, for codex Bezae omits the articles leaving the text *gunaikon proton.* But even this reduction can mean "leading women," or even "women of the best social standing." The women were Greek, rather than Jewish, though they had become believers in God and adherents to the synagogue. While it must be admitted that the precise meaning of Luke's adjective "chief" is unclear, there is significance in the fact that he drew special attention to them and that their influence would be felt both by their status and their number.[15]

VI. BEREA

Paul and Silas were sent out of Thessalonica by night following the riot and the assault of Jason to the town of Berea some forty miles away.[16] Here they found people more ready to accept their doctrine, in that they searched the scriptures daily to determine the validity of what they heard preached. Of the many converted in that place, Luke makes special mention of the honorable Greek women. As in Thessalonica, women seem to play a prominent role in the social affairs of Berea, no doubt reflecting the history of Macedonian women. Also as in Thessalonica, Paul found a great number of God-fearers among the Greeks, and those accepted his doctrine in great numbers, both men and women. But Luke's description of these women as honorable is especially noteworthy. Lenski concludes that the article added to the adjective, plus the fact that the women are mentioned before the others, indicates first, that the women converted were more in number than the men; and second, that they were of greater community influence and social status than the men.[17]

Several scholars have observed the apparent anti-feminist tendency of the writer of Codex Bezae.[18] This reviser represents the western textual tradition dating back to the second century, and clearly reveals the trend of thought among his contemporaries by rephrasing the received text of Acts 17:12 to read: "and many of the Greeks and men and women of high standing believed." The smoother reading serves to lessen any importance given women in Luke's account of the conversion at Berea, and proves to be a typical alteration of Bezae in Acts.

Menoud suggests that the anti-feminist trend in Bezae was more or less general in the last decades of the first century, but was not among the major concerns of the western recension as a whole.[19] However, accumulative evidence strongly points to a concerted effort on the part of traditionalists spanning at least two centuries to thwart any movements which might have arisen out of the Christian message to elevate the status of women, and to obscure any teachings in the New Testament which might give support to such a movement. Their efforts were successful.

VII. ATHENS

At Athens, principal city of Achaia and cultural center of the ancient Greek world, Paul became involved in a verbal exchange with a group of Stoic and Epicurean philosophers who escorted him to the Areopagus to hear his doctrine. Luke's account concludes with the mention of two converts by name, "Dionysius, the Areopagite, and a woman named Damaris,"[20] and certain others. The name Damaris is apparently unknown elsewhere in Greek literature, and is thought by some to be a corruption of a common name Damalis, meaning "heifer." It could have been a nickname worn by any one of the thousands of hetaerae, a special class of prostitute in ancient Greece. The hetaerae had special social liberties, and many were known for intellectual pursuits. Some scholars insist that she was an aristocrat, a woman of consequence, and of considerable importance to the early church in Athens. In all fairness, this is all speculation.

However, of special interest is that Codex Bezae omits the phrase "and a woman named Damaris," which can easily be explained as an accidental omission by a weary copyist. But in view of the anti-feminist alterations already noted, it would seem that this omission was deliberate and intentional in an effort to obscure the truth: that women in the early church enjoyed honor and influence uncharacteristic of their day.

VIII. CORINTH

Paul's visit to Corinth lasted at least two years, during which time a sizable congregation was established. The most notable converts were a husband and wife who shared Paul's profession, and with whom he worked and lived during the early months of his stay in that city. Their names were Aquila and Priscilla.[21] This couple proved to be dedicated Christians, capable of expounding the scriptures and worthy of commendation as laborers in the gospel.

But of the two, there is reason to believe that Priscilla was the more capable and the more zealous in the faith. Bruce, Harnack and others consider it possible that this couple had been converted elsewhere and were foundation members of the Roman Church.[22] The couple later accompanied Paul to Ephesus, where they settled.[23] Priscilla will be discussed fully in the next section as a representative of that city.

Other significant women in the Corinthian church are the prophetesses of I Corinthians 11, and those rebuked for speaking in I Corinthians 14. These likewise will be dealt with in other sections.

A women worthy of mention at this point is Chloe. In I Corinthians 1:11 Paul writes: "For I have been informed concerning you, my brethren, by Chloe's people, that there are quarrels among you." The name Chloe was an epithet of Demeter, and she probably was of the freedman class.[24] The expression "Chloe's people" (upo ton Chloes) has been understood variously, but nearly all narrow the interpretation down to two possible categories: either slaves or relatives. There is the possibility that she resided in Ephesus, and that her people had visited Corinth and returned with a report of dissension among the Christians. Mention of her name may have intensified the situation were she a current member of the Corinthian church. Nevertheless, she was known to them, and the mention of her name by Paul suggests some degree of respect among that body of Christians.

IX. EPHESUS

After a short period in Ephesus Paul bade farewell to Priscilla and Aquila and made his way back to Antioch, leaving them to carry on the work. Priscilla's name presents considerable problems; first, because it appears in two forms, and second, because it is often mentioned before the name of Aquila. "Prisca," which appears in the epistles, seems to be the more formal and perhaps indicates a relatively high social class. English versions do not consistently translate the name; for example, in I Corinthians 16:19 the Authorized Version translates priska "Priscilla." Priscilla, the more common name, appears in all other references and is probably the name used by her friends. The fact that in two of Luke's three references to the couple Priscilla's name is given first might suggest her prominence.[25] Again the western reviser reveals his anti-feminist persuasion by attempting to reduce the prominence of Priscilla. In both verses 18 and 26 of Acts 18 the western text reverses the order of names to read Aquila and Priscilla, and elsewhere makes various alterations including the insertion of the name of Aquila without including Priscilla. According to Metzger:

The unusual order, the wife before the husband, must be accepted as original, for there was always a tendency among scribes to change the unusual to the usual. In the case of Priscilla and Aquila, however, it was customary in the early church to refer to her before her husband.[26]

Paul himself mentions her first in two epistles.[27] Therefore, it is reasonable to assume that when Apollos arrived in Ephesus it was Priscilla who took the initiative "expounding unto him the way of God more perfectly." Without a doubt the historian Luke intended to leave that impression.

Various conjectures have been made as to why Priscilla was listed first. Chrysostom, representing an early Christian tradition, was convinced that she was "more zealous and more fruitful" in her dedication to the Lord.[28] Bruce, however, thinks that the name represented a noble Roman family bearing the title *gens Prisca*.[29] Exploration by De Rossi in an ancient catacomb, the *Coeneterium Priscillae*, revealed that originally the tomb contained the body of Acilius Glabrio, a Roman Christian who was consul with Trajan around A.D. 91. It was further discovered that the name of the females in the *Acilion gens*, verified by inscriptions, was Prisca or Priscilla.[30] The fact that a catacomb had been opened to Christians, and that Acilius Glabrio was a believer, indicates that the lineage must have included numerous Christians. If this line of reasoning is correct, and Priscilla was of the Acilian family, it is unlikely that such a noble woman would have married a Jewish tentmaker of Pontus. It is possible then, that she was a freedwoman of the Acilian family and bore the traditional name of females in that lineage.

There is no question about the extensive involvement of Priscilla and Aquila in the work of the church in various places. After the disciples separated themselves from the synagogue, the home of this couple served as central headquarters and principal meeting place for the new Christian community at Ephesus. Paul later calls them his "fellow workers" in Christ, a term which no doubt emerged from the workshop vernacular of Paul in application to their joint efforts in proclaiming the Gospel. Paul further states that they had "laid down their necks" for him.[31] This expression was common in Paul's day and conveyed the idea of standing beside him in the face of great opposition. For this Paul expresses his gratitude and that of the Gentile churches. There may have been occasions in which Priscilla and Aquila literally risked their lives for the sake of the work, and particularly to ensure Paul's personal safety. In view of the fierce persecution of Christians in various quarters there is no reason to think that Paul exaggerated in this instance.[32]

Harnack was the first to suggest Priscilla as the author of Hebrews, a theory which might explain why early church tradition left the author anonymous. History of textual transmission in the late first and early second centuries, mentioned earlier, lends support to Harnack's theory. Guthrie summarizes that view in the statement: "The name of a woman as author would have been so prejudicial to its acceptance that it would be omitted for reasons of prudence."[33] Little else has been offered in her favor, however, and most scholars reject the theory. Of all those suggested as author of Hebrews, the most likely is Apollos. But it is significant that Priscilla is credited with the conversion of this Alexandrian Jew, who in turn may have penned such an outstanding work.

In summary, evidence is striking that Priscilla was an outstanding individual in the work of the early church. Both Paul and Luke credit her with higher recognition than her husband. It would be difficult to state categorically, as some writers do, that her work was of a public evangelistic nature. But Priscilla was certainly an example of individuality and self-assertion on the part of first-century Christian women.

X. CENCHREA

Cenchrea was a small community comprising the eastern port of Corinth on the Saronic Gulf. The church there was probably founded by Paul during his first visit to Corinth. Here Paul shaved his head in observance of a vow he had taken prior to leaving for Ephesus, and here also resided a Christian woman named Phoebe. She is the first name mentioned in Paul's extensive salutations at the end of his epistle to the Romans, and nothing is known of her except what is stated in this single reference:

> I commend to you our sister Phoebe, who is a servant of the church which is at Cenchrea; that you receive her in the Lord in a manner worthy of the saints, and that you help her in whatever matter she may have need of you; for she herself has also been a helper of many, and of myself as well.[34]

There is some disagreement as to whether the sixteenth chapter of Romans was originally sent to Rome or to Ephesus. But many reputable scholars hold that it is in its correct place at the close, and that Phoebe was the bearer of the entire epistle. Paul's commendation of her, expressed by the term *sunistanai*, can be taken to represent her formal introduction to the Christian community. Apparently such letters of recommendation were common in the early church. But in this case the bearer of the letter is not transferring her home to Rome, or Paul would have said something like, "Receive her unto yourselves." Instead she is going there on business, perhaps for the church.

Phoebe is called by Paul "our sister," a common New Testament term signifying her union with the Apostle and fellow believers in the faith. Her name means "bright" or "radiant" and is the old epithet of the moon goddess Artemis, sister of Apollos (Phoebus). One might expect such former worshippers of pagan deities to change their names upon conversion, but there is little evidence of this occurring among those mentioned in the New Testament.

The masculine *diakonos* is thought by some to be used by Paul in a technical sense, indicating that Phoebe held an official position in the church at Cenchrea similar to that of the seven appointed in the church at Jerusalem.[35] She therefore would have belonged to that class of church servants indicated by *diakonia* in Romans 12:7 and by *diakonoi* in Philippians 1:1. Concerning the first-century order of deaconesses more will be said later.

The term translated "helper," *prostatis*, had a wide and varied use in Paul's day, but most often denoted a technical or official status of "patron," much like the Latin *patronus*. According to some, the masculine form was the title of a citizen in Athens who took charge of the interests of clients and persons without civic rights. In general the term describes an official guardian, champion or legal representative. In Hellenistic communities the word also described a patron, and ancient epitaphs reveal that in some synagogues a particular woman might be honored with the title "Mistress" or "Matron" in return for outstanding charitable service. In heathen religious societies, especially among the poorer classes, wealthy and influential individuals were often appointed as patrons.

It is possible, therefore, that Paul used the term *prostatis* in a technical sense, and that Phoebe was the patroness of either the seaport Cenchrea or of the small and struggling church there. Her visit to Rome would have been to solicit financial aid. This possibility is strengthened by Paul's poetic admonition to "assist her," *parastete*, as she has been "the assistant (patron) of many," *prostatis pollon*. Various scholars venture to speculate concerning the ministry of Phoebe to Paul, an unrecorded incident, suggesting that she had cared for him while he was ill at Cenchrea, that the church in Cenchrea met in Phoebe's home, that she was known for assisting brethren landing at that port, and that she was a widow. But none of this can be substantiated.

While little can be said with certainty about Phoebe's official status, either social or religious, it is clear that she was an outstanding woman in Paul's estimation and that she was of great value to the church. The above-mentioned speculation is certainly plausible and has much to its credit. Phoebe is the only named member of the church in Cenchrea, and certainly deserves credit as one of the outstanding Christians of the apostolic church.

XI. ROME

In the sixteenth chapter of Romans, six of the twenty-seven people saluted by name are women, and two additional women are mentioned though unnamed. The first two are Priscilla and Phoebe, who have been discussed already.

The third woman mentioned is Mary, to whom Paul sends greetings and whom he identifies as having bestowed much labor on the Christians at Rome.[36] Although there is a textual variant concerning the spelling of the name, the Jewish form *Mariam* carries the greater weight of evidence.[37] Most authorities therefore assume her to be a Jewess, and of unusual prominence in the Roman Christian community, indicated by the proximity of her name to those of Phoebe, Priscilla and Aquila in Paul's salutations.

Another variant concerning Mary is worthy of mention. The accepted text reads "Mary who bestowed much labor on us." But upon the overwhelming testimony of manuscripts, the original certainly read "on you," strongly suggests Mary's service to the entire church, either during an epidemic, an economic crisis or in various general ways. But if the Authorized Version is correct it might reflect the role Mary played, along with Prisca, Aquila and others, in supporting Paul's work at an earlier stage, and perhaps in ministering to those who surrounded him. After that Mary went to Rome.[38] While it does seem reasonable that Paul was aware of Mary's godly service by personal contact as with others mentioned, it is equally possible that he had heard of her work among the Roman Christians merely by reputation, having never met her nor visited that community.

Farther along in Paul's personal greetings appear the names of Tryphena and Tryphosa, "who labor in the Lord."[39] These two women are generally thought to be sisters, possibly twins, considering the similarity of names. The two names come from the same Greek verb, *truphan*, meaning "to live luxuriously." Walls translates the names as "Delicate" and "Dainty," respectively.[40] The former sister is definitely not to be identified with the Tryphena, daughter of Polemon I of Pontus and mother of three kings, mentioned in the apocryphal *Acts of Paul and Thecla*.

In the same verse, Paul salutes Persis: "the beloved, who labored much in the Lord." The term "beloved" is used elsewhere, especially by Paul, to denote a general affection held by fellow Christians for certain individuals.[41] Usually the term is applied to well-known and meritorious Christians, endeared to the entire community of believers.

These four women, greeted separately by Paul, are drawn together by a single term employed in each case to describe the Christian service for which they were commended. The word *kopian*, translated "labor," appears in classical Greek meaning "to grow tired" or "to become weary of good things." In secular and Septuagint Greek the meaning was "to tire" or "to wear oneself out," either in battle, at work, by mental strain, or even "to swelter from heat."[42] In the Gospels the word appears with much the same meaning, exemplified by Luke's discussion of the fishermen who "toiled all night" on Gennesaret with no catch.[43] Deissman refers to a tombstone epitaph in Asia Minor, describing the "labor" of a humble gardener, and the word *kopian* is used.[44] However, Hauck says that in the New Testament there appears a distinctive use of the term for the Christian labor in and for the community. In the writing of Paul the word appears nineteen times and relates primarily to the agonizing toil, perhaps beyond the call of duty, in which he and certain fellow workers persisted for the cause of Jesus Christ. As Hauck points out, the term in Paul's usage relates primarily to "missionary and pastoral work,"[45] which is strong evidence for their prominence and the respect they must have commanded in spiritual matters.

However, a more honest approach to the interpretation of Paul's terminology here might be to determine first the nature of work generally done by women in the apostolic church, and then to presuppose that kind of labor as implied in the term *kopian*. Much physical labor was required of women in the early Christian community in the form of cooking, sewing, medical care, tending of orphans and the aged, and informal instruction. The term "labor" need not imply public preaching or pastoral work. This is not to say that women did not participate in preaching; only that such activities cannot be proved from the terminology used here.

In Romans 16:7 Paul salutes Andronicus and Junia(s), whom he identifies as "my kinsmen, and my fellow prisoners, who are outstanding among the apostles, who also were in Christ before me." The expression "my kinsmen" probably means "fellow countrymen" rather than "relatives."[46] But "my fellow prisoners" can be taken literally. At some stage in his work thus far Paul had been imprisoned for preaching the Gospel. The earliest was at Philippi (Acts 16:1), although numerous possibilities exist for longer or shorter periods in prison including Ephesus, Caesarea, and Jerusalem. Andronicus and Junia(s) either had accompanied him on one or more occasions, or had been imprisoned elsewhere for the same alleged offenses. There is no question that these two fellow prisoners of Paul were Christians before his own conversion.

The first of two problems with Andronicus and Junia(s) is that there is no means of determining whether the name of the latter is masculine or feminine. The word *Iounian* might be a contraction of the masculine *Iounianos* which, though unusual, is the same in construction as Patrobas, Hermas or Plympas. It could also be the feminine Junia, which was a very common Roman name for women. If Junia(s) is a woman, then she is probably the wife or sister of Andronicus.

The second problem involves the interpretation of the adjectival phrase "outstanding among the apostles." Chrysostom understood this to mean that the couple were actually termed apostles by the early church and in that capacity had achieved considerable fame. Moreover, Chrysostom found no difficulty with the idea of a female apostle:

> And indeed to be apostles at all is a great thing. But to be even among these of note, just consider what a great encomium this is! But they were of note owing to their works and to their achievements. Oh! how great is the devotion of this woman, that she should be even considered worthy of the appellation of apostle.[47]

Certain modern writers who favor greater feminine roles in the church today appeal to the above comment of Chrysostom for support. Dodd, for example, says "Chrysostom . . . saw no difficulty in a woman apostle, nor need we."[48] But Dodd seems to make a distinction in terms not made by Chrysostom. The ancient writer understood Junia to have held an office entitled "apostle," but Dodd states that all those "sent out" as missionaries to proclaim the Gospel also bore the unofficial title "apostle," as did Barnabas. Therefore, to call Junia an apostle might not make her equal with the Twelve, but would give her the status of "sent-forth evangelist." But even this is beyond the status many are willing to acknowledge.

There are several reasons for rejecting the above treatment of the phrase "outstanding among the Apostles." First, the most natural interpretation of "apostles" is "the Twelve," or at least those who remained of that group designated apostles from the ascension of Christ. Of the eighty instances of the term *apostolos* in the New Testament only four can be identified with someone other than the official group known as the Twelve (or the Eleven).[49] Second, the passage in question is most logically understood to say that Andronicus and Junia(s) were highly esteemed by and well known to the apostles, not that they were themselves noted apostles. Third, numerous scholars feel strongly that Junia(s) was a man.[50] For these reasons great caution must be exercised in suggesting Junia(s) as an example of female evangelism or apostleship in the early church.

Nevertheless, if the name did indicate a woman she is worthy of commendation in that her name was well known to the apostles for her faith, godly works and perseverence in trial.

Two unnamed women appear among the recipients of Paul's salutations. The first is the mother of Rufus.[51] Paul describes Rufus as "chosen in the Lord," probably meaning "distinguished in Christian service," or "an outstanding Christian." The name Rufus appears elsewhere only in Mark 15:21, there identified as the son of Simon of Cyrene and brother of Alexander. Though Simon is mentioned in all three Synoptics, his sons, who probably outlived him by many years and became leaders in the church, are named by Mark only. In view of Mark's traditional association with Peter in Rome, and his writing of a Gospel account for a Roman audience, it seems natural for the name of Rufus to appear both in Mark's Gospel and in Paul's letter to the Romans.[52] The mother of Rufus, now probably a widow, had at some time showed Paul the care and affection of a mother, and here Paul salutes her with the tender respect of a son.

In verse fifteen of this chapter Paul salutes a group undoubtedly representing a house-church within the broader scope of the church at Rome. The addition of "all the saints with them" suggests a large group, as does "all the brethren which are with them" concerning another group mentioned in verse 14. The five mentioned specifically seem to be the leaders of the comparatively small congregation meeting in a particular section of the city, but Paul does not state that the church met in their house as he did in the case of Priscilla and Aquila. Therefore, it is difficult to determine the relationship of the group, although scholars generally regard Julia and Philologus to be husband and wife, and their daughter, sister of Nereus, is not named. However, if the *Iounian* of verse seven can be taken as masculine, then it seems that *Ioulian* (also accusative) should be rendered Julian instead of Julia. Yet scholars insist that the latter is among the most common of Roman female names.[53]

One other woman can be associated with the church at Rome, though her name appears only in II Timothy 4:21, where Paul sends greetings to the young evangelist from all the Christians where he was, including Pudens, Linus and Claudia. According to tradition Paul wrote this letter to Timothy from prison in Rome soon before his martyrdom. If this be the case, then without question Claudia can be associated with the church in Rome. Her name suggests imperial lineage, although she is likely to have been a slave of the household of Claudius.[54] Her name is given in the *Apostolic Constitutions* as the mother of Linus, who is thought to be the bishop of Rome, and another tradition identifies her with Claudia Rufina, wife of Aulus Pudens, who was a friend of Martial.[55] But Lightfoot, after a thorough study of related traditions, rejects all theories identifying Claudia as the wife of Pudens or mother of Linus.[56] Therefore, nothing definite can be determined about Claudia and those mentioned with her, except that they were personally acquainted with Paul and Timothy and were of high esteem to the church in Rome.

XII. LAODICEA

In Colossians 4:15 Paul mentions another individual whose gender is disputed. The Authorized Version reads: "Salute the brethren which are in Laodicea, and Nymphas, the church which is in their house." Apparently

the word *numphan* can be accented so as to represent either a masculine
or a feminine name, without changing the spelling. The uncertainty of the
gender led to manuscript variations in the possessive pronoun between
autes and *auton*, and much later when copyists included *adelphous* in the
reference the reading *auton* appeared. Metzger and others favor the
feminine name and pronoun, primarily on the strength of manuscript
witnesses.[57] Lightfoot and others reject the feminine name, which they say
is Doric and is in this reference highly improbable.[58]

It seems that nothing definite can be determined about the person
whom Paul calls Nympha(s), and further discussion of the question would
add nothing of worth to the picture of women in the apostolic church. It
has already been determined that various women opened their homes to
Christian travelers and provided meeting places for the church in their
vicinity. If Nympha(s) was a woman this may have been her primary contribution to the work of the church.

XIII. COLOSSAE

Paul begins his letter to Philemon with the salutation: "Paul, a prisoner
of Christ Jesus, and Timothy our brother, to Philemon our beloved brother
and fellow worker, and to Apphia our sister, and to Archippus our fellow
soldier, and to the church in your house." Here is another house-church
with several members known and loved by Paul. Since Onesimus, the
runaway slave of Philemon, is associated with the church in Colossae it is
commonly thought that Philemon also resided there.[59] For the personal
nature of this letter Paul drops the authoritative title of apostle and uses a
number of affectionate terms, no doubt to soften Philemon to the requests
contained in the letter. Perhaps it was during Paul's long sojourn at Ephesus
that Philemon had labored with him in the Gospel, as well as Archippus,
but the details of their association are unknown. They are undoubtedly
pillars in the church.

Between the names of Philemon and Archippus appears that of Apphia. Some manuscripts describe her as "the beloved," while others
substitute "our sister." The preponderance of ancient authority favors the
latter, and it is sure to pertain to their spiritual relationship rather than a
physical one.

Concerning the identity of Apphia it is a safe inference from the connection of the names that Apphia was the wife of Philemon, and Archippus
was probably their son. Contrary to the opinion of many commentators
the name Apphia seems to be Phrygian rather than Roman. The nature of
the letter to this household is domestic rather than doctrinal, and for this
reason the greetings suggest little concerning the status of those mentioned

in the church. But the fact that Paul greeted each by name, and that the church met in their home, can be regarded as complimentary of the character and devotion of the matron of the house, Apphia.

XIV. ICONIUM

One other woman in the apostolic church worthy of mention is Thecla, who appears not in the New Testament but in *The Acts of Paul and Thecla.* This apocryphal book was ascribed by Tertullian to a presbyter of Asia who allegedly compiled the work out of love for Paul. Thecla was converted by Paul at Iconium and is credited with preaching the word. Sir William Ramsay says: "Thecla became the type of female Christian teacher, preacher, and baptizer, and her story was quoted as early as the second century as justification of the right of women to teach and baptize."[60] But in another work Ramsay speaks of the story of St. Thecla as an Iconian legend adopted, with heretical features toned down, first by ascetic sects and then by those who advocated the social rights of women.[61] Therefore the legend of Thecla, much like the brief references to the work of individual women in the New Testament, raises many questions and offers little solid evidence for any specific leadership role for women. However, Thecla was a real individual, and seems to have been an extraordinary individual in the apostolic church. And the possibility of her work as an evangelist being toned down in history by anti-feminists is more plausible than the suggestion that feminists exaggerated her status to promote female liberation. There is really no evidence of the latter in this period.

In spite of the sketchy details, evidence examined in this chapter is sufficent to indicate the prominence of women in the early apostolic church. From the time of its establishment the church had a place for the talents and energies of women, including some form of teaching or proclamation of the Gospel. Among the examples cited there is some evidence for female evangelists, though sketchy and inconclusive, but women are commended openly for various kinds of labor in the cause of Christ, perhaps at times straining contemporary standards of propriety. Yet, there is revealed in these examples a marked elevation in the status of women in the church as compared to that in contemporary secular society. Textual alterations cited indicate considerable prejudice against women among certain copyists and revisers in the second century, and whatever trends there may have been in the early church in favor of women were strongly opposed by traditionalists who had the means to turn the tide.

3. Female Officers in the Early Christian Church

From the previous chapter it should be clear that women played a significant role in the work of the early church, and many stood out individually for their efforts. A question arises, however, concerning official positions of authority and leadership. Numerous titles and roles emerge from scripture and church history which point to the existence of certain female officers, including deaconesses and enrolled widows.

Organization in the early church seems to have developed at a varied rate, depending upon needs and circumstances of individual congregations. A number of modern biblical scholars have held that church offices appeared only in the second and third centuries, harmonizing with late dates suggested by liberal theologians for various New Testament books. Admittedly, both Acts and the Pauline Epistles, with the possible exception of the Pastorals, exhibit ecclesiastical polity in a rudimentary state in which offices are neither clearly nor permanently defined. Terminology is inconsistent, the same word describing general functions of church leaders in some places, in others denoting official titles and still in others describing qualities and functions of individuals not holding any official position.[1] The term "office" is not used in the New Testament to describe church leadership, and may in reality convey a concept of leadership that is more structured and authoritative than was actually the case in the early church. The roles prompted by the Holy Spirit and enumerated by Paul in I Corinthians 12:28 include apostles, prophets and teachers, and those which Paul states were set in the church by God to build it up (Ephesians 4:11) were apostles, prophets, evangelists, pastors and teachers. Of these scholars generally see apostleship as a unique role limited to those initially sent out by Christ, and including Paul. The prophets were also a special category identifiable by charismatic gifts, and teachers are thought of in broad general terms with no official capacity.

There were two leadership roles which are generally considered to be offices and which appear to be completely functional before the close of the first century, both established by apostolic authority as local congregations matured.

The first such office is that of the elder (or presbyter, *presbuteros*), also called bishop (or overseer, *episkopos*) or pastor (shepherd, *poimen*).[2] Although these and perhaps other terms are more descriptive than titular and may vary with locality, they represent a single office which arose naturally from the Jewish concept of community and synagogue elders. Peter is careful to point out, perhaps in reflection of Jesus' own words to the disciples, that his role is one of gentle shepherding and example, rather than authoritative rule.[3] Nevertheless, the congregation is encouraged to submit to their guidance.

The secondary officers are called deacons (or servants, ministers, *diakonoi*).[4] The origin of the deaconate is commonly sought in the selection of the Seven at Jerusalem, a view which has found favor with scholars in general since the early church fathers.[5] These seven were selected from among the Jerusalem Christians, and were appointed by the apostles to "serve tables" so that the Twelve could "continue steadfastly in prayer and in the ministry of the word." A situation had arisen concerning benevolent services of the church, specifically to widows, requiring the attention of capable men given official responsibility in that area. Hence, the work assigned on this occasion is recognized to be a ministry, or a service, described in Greek by the term *diakonia*. The term "deacon" does not appear in this passage, however, at least not in reference to the Seven, and the qualifications do not parallel those prescribed by Paul in I Timothy 3:8–12. Furthermore, Luke's record has Stephen and Philip immediately appearing before the public as miracle workers and evangelists, rather than carrying out any form of benevolent ministry as deacons. The Seven can be called deacons only in the sense that they were appointed to a benevolent ministry in the church, and that they became the assistants or helpers of those holding a superior office, in this case the apostles. The office later defined as the deaconate seems to have its practical origin here.

The first use of the term *diakonos* as an official title is by Paul in his letter to the Philippians, around A.D. 59–60, but the reference gives no details as to qualifications.[6] By this date there appears to be a fixed order of officials in the church at Philippi, for the apostle addresses himself "to all the saints in Christ Jesus that are at Philippi, with the bishops and deacons." A few years later, in his first letter to Timothy, Paul outlined certain guidelines for selecting both deacons and elders. Combining the root meaning of *diakonos* with the personal requirements to hold such an office, it appears that deacons served as assistants to the elders, ministering to the material needs of the church and working in all areas of physical Christian service. Deacons also were generally younger men than elders, perhaps being Christians for a shorter period, and one might infer that the deaconate was a proving ground for later service in the episcopate.

It is difficult to state to what degree deacons should be thought of as officers of the church, since the term means "servant" or "minister" and is used by Paul of himself and Timothy in their respective roles as apostle and evangelist. Some state that in such cases the term had a non-official sense, but it might be that it was never intended by Paul to carry the kind of official connotation it has today. Perhaps it was a broad general term appropriately applied to anyone delegated a service task or role in the church, regardless of its nature.

Whether or not this was the case the term has a bearing on some kind of role, office or ministry in the early church which involved women, and whatever information can be extrapolated from external sources can only enhance our understanding of relevant biblical texts.

I. DEACONESSES

Although the offices discussed or implied by New Testament writers are almost totally occupied by men, there are hints that certain women in the early church likewise held official positions, including that of deaconess. On this subject thoughts immediately return to Phoebe, whom Paul described as "a servant (*diakonos*) of the church which is at Cenchrea."[7] The initial difficulty lies in determining whether the term deacon (servant) is used in an official sense or simply to describe the Christian service rendered spontaneously by Phoebe on behalf of the community. The form of the Greek term is masculine, and cannot correctly be rendered "deaconess." Moulton and Milligan indicate that according to papyri evidence the term had a technical application to holders of various offices in social and religious life of the pagan world.[8] There is also ample evidence of deaconesses in pre-Christian Judaism as assistants in various Levitical functions.[9] Furthermore, in some of the mystery religions there were both male and female *diakonoi*. On this basis, it appears that the way was prepared by the earlier secular and religious application of the term for a technical use in the church concerning female workers. Scholars such as Dodd feel certain that whatever the deacons at Philippi were Phoebe was at Cenchrae.[10] We have no reason to think that the term carries any less weight here than when elsewhere Paul applies it to himself, to Tychicus, Timothy and Epaphras in which places most versions read "minister."[11] The word is the same, and whether translated "deacon" or "minister" it assigns to Phoebe a status many are reluctant to recognize.

Another possible reference to deaconesses in the early church is I Timothy 3:11, which reads: "Women in like manner must be serious, not

slanderers, but temperate, faithful in all things." The context of this statement is the qualities desirable in candidates for elders and deacons. Verse
eleven is immediately preceded by a list of characteristics desirable in
deacons, which most naturally indicates that *gunaika* (women) must in
some way parallel the above-mentioned categories. The Authorized Version renders this term "wives," which leads the reader to assume that certain
qualities were demanded also of the wives of candidates for either elder or
deacon or both. This translation clearly reflects the seventeenth-century
Catholic attitude toward women, and appears to be intentionally mis-
leading.

The absence of an article with the noun in this case suggests that elders,
deacons and women in this context were categories of service the nature of
which demanded maturity and exemplary character in those so appointed.
Had the passage been intended to describe wives of deacons and elders one
would expect to find such characteristics as subjection to their husbands,
child-rearing and hospitality as in Titus 2:4–5, and it would have been simple enough for the writer to have used the possessive pronoun "their" to
make himself clear. The term *osautos* (likewise) is customarily used to introduce the second and third entities in a series and would seem to place
these three groups in categories of similar nature. The same thing is suggested by the verb combination introducing each category, suggesting what
qualities the candidates must have. The fact that Paul inserts the women
in the middle of his discussion of deacons suggests that their work is similar,
and on a plane not quite the same as that of elders. In general whatever is
said here about deacons would apply to the women, at least in principle,
for their work is much the same.

The qualities expected of these women further indicates the office or
ministry of deaconess. Of the four adjectival expressions used here two are
found among the qualifications for elders and deacons, and the other two
are paralleled roughly.

As far as can be determined none of the Ante-Nicene fathers make
reference to Phoebe as a deaconess. But Pliny, a Roman noble in the service
of the Emperor Trajan, wrote a letter in A.D. 112 reporting on an investigation he had conducted among Bithynian churches. Admittedly, Pliny does
not appear to be well informed concerning Christian beliefs, for he speaks
of torturing two women in an attempt to extract information from them
concerning their religion. Whether hoping to find evidence of cannibalism,
incest or some other lurid crime we do not know, but what we learn is that
they were recognized by the church in some way as deaconesses. Pliny
writes:

> I judged it so much the more necessary to extract the real truth, with
> the assistance of fortune, from two female slaves, who were styled

deaconesses; but I could discover nothing more than depraved and excessive superstition.[12]

Again, the Latin term which Pliny used was *ministrae*, which could have
been rendered "servants" or "ministers." In either case the typical New
Testament use of the term suggests some kind of official status.

Further evidence appears in various works of Clement of Alexandria,
written in the late second century. In his treatment of I Corinthians 9:5
where Paul discusses the right of apostles to "lead about a wife who is a
sister" Clement makes reference to the role of deaconesses. Although his interpretation of this particular passage seems incorrect, he does express an
awareness of deaconesses in the early church, which he defines as assisting
the apostles and taking care of the ministry by which they were able to
bring the doctrine of the Lord into women's apartments without suspicion
of blame.

Clement also discusses the role of deaconesses in his *Stromata*. Therein
he says that the service they render has to do with showing hospitality, service deeds related to housekeeping for others and implies various supportive
roles in teaching and evangelism. The noted lexicographer Lampe
understands this material by Clement to pertain to *de diaconissa
primitiva*.[13]

Other than the references of Pliny and Clement, there is silence concerning deaconesses till the late third century. The silence is broken by a
very lengthy treatment of the subject in the *Apostolic Constitutions*, a compilation of Syrian material from various sources. Of this collection the
seventh book, known as the *Didascalia Apostolorum*, or *Teaching*, dates
from the third century. The remainder of the *Constitutions* is thought to
have been written no later than the fifth century, and no earlier than the
fourth. In these works the office of deaconess is clearly defined, and appears
to be a prominent feature of church organization.

Few authorities attempt to explain the long literary silence on the subject between the New Testament and the *Apostolic Constitutions*, but the
office either existed continuously from the apostolic era with little occasion
for mention, or was suddenly revived in the third century due to changing
needs in the church. Either explanation presupposes an order of
deaconesses in the first-century church. This is not to suggest that it did not
change or become more technically defined. It is certain that all church
offices went through considerable evolution after the apostolic era, in some
cases drifting away from original conceptual intent. Schaff recognizes that
in post-apostolic times the bishop came to be elevated above the presbyter,
the presbyter developed into the priest, and the deacon "became the first of
three orders in the ministry and a stepping-stone to the priesthood."[14]
Observing these and other significant changes in church dogma it becomes

difficult to accept that the third-century order of deaconesses was maintained unaltered from the apostolic church.

According to the *Apostolic Constitutions*, deaconesses were ordained by the laying on of hands, as were deacons. In the case of a deacon, however, a prayer was made that he might achieve a higher standing, no doubt referring to the eldership.[15] At this time, it seems that deaconess was the highest office in the church obtainable by a woman. Their ministry involved numerous practical duties in the daily life of the community and in certain religious ceremonies, but they appear to be confined almost totally to caring for the needs of other women, benevolence, keeping orphans and teaching. They assisted women with baptism by keeping the doors, anointing and receiving after immersion, but not performing the baptism itself.[16] They also stood by the doors of the worship assembly to keep order among the women.[17] Deaconesses served as intermediaries between lay women and other church officers,[18] and widows were expected to hold them in high esteem as they would male officials.[19]

But strangely enough, the *Teaching*, which is the oldest portion of the *Constitutions*, makes no mention of deaconesses or *any* female officers in its section concerning the ordination of church officials.[20] This might indicate that deaconess only came to be a recognized office in the eastern church in the early fourth century, after the *Teaching* was completed. In support of this suggestion is the fact that the first appearance of the word *diakonissa* in Christian literature is in the canons of the Council of Nicea, A.D. 325, and even there cautions are issued to the effect that deaconesses should not be considered as among the clergy. In the *Apostolic Constitutions* this rather advanced and technical term appears only in Book VIII, which is the latest of the materials dating from the fourth to early fifth centuries.[21]

After this era references to deaconesses are more plentiful, and most writers assume the order to have originated in the New Testament continuing up to their own day. Chrysostom, writing around A.D. 381–398, makes the first patristic reference to alleged deaconesses in I Timothy 3:11:

> Some have thought that this is said of women generally, but it is not so, for why should he introduce anything about women to interfere with the subject? He is speaking of those who hold the rank of deaconess.[22]

It is difficult if not impossible to trace accurately the changes in definition of the role of deaconesses as well as the changes in attitude toward them. But it does appear that in the western church a strong anti-feminist movement occurred, visible in various western texts of which Codex Bezae is a prime example. By the fourth century restrictions were being placed on the appointment of deaconesses, especially with regard to their ordination.

The sacramental concepts associated with ordination in the minds of church officials set it above the worthiness of women. At about this time also special orders of nuns were developing, and their austerity and separation from association with ordinary people made them more acceptable to current theology. Therefore nuns gradually took over the role of deaconesses, and the latter disappeared from the western church by the eighth century and from the eastern church by the eleventh century.

II. WIDOWS

Another category of women in the early church which might be thought of as an office pertains to widowhood. But as in the case of deaconesses, evidence for such an office is the subject of much debate.

Widows in the Apostolic Church

Very early in church history widows became the recipients of special consideration. Luke writes:

> Now at this time while the disciples were increasing in number, a complaint arose on the part of the Hellenistic Jews against the native Hebrews, because their widows were being overlooked in the daily serving of food.[23]

Throughout the history of Israel it was recognized that the plight of a widow, or for that matter any woman living independently, could be very bitter. For this cause widows, along with orphans, were recognized as a socially deprived class requiring special protection and maintenance. But those widows who joined the Christian community were no doubt thought of as unworthy of assistance, having forsaken Moses, and were cut off from aid provided by Jewish law from the *ketubbah* or from the Temple treasury.[24]

From the start the Jerusalem church recognized and willingly shouldered the responsibility for ministering to the needs of widows among its number. But it appears that some form of discrimination occurred which met with formal protest. Conflict between Hellenistic and nationalistic Jews in Palestine is well documented in history, and in the New Testament religio-political factions such as the Sadducees and Pharisees are mentioned frequently. That tension between them would carry over into the Christian community is quite understandable, but it is unfortunate that widows bore the brunt of it in this case. The accusation was lodged that somehow the widows of Hellenistic background were being overlooked.

In response to the problem the apostles encourage the church to select several responsible men to be appointed over this special work of benevolence. The selection which ensued yields seven names commonly thought of as the first deacons. They are not actually called such, but the cognate *diakonia* appears several times in the discussion and is translated "service" or "ministry."

It is worthy of note that some scholars see in this account the beginnings of a primitive order of widows who in return for financial support devoted their time to prayer, meditation and good works. In fact, some believe that the office of widow and deaconess to be the same, and that the ministry here was actually performed by widows rather than their being the recipients of benevolence. The problem which came to the apostles' attention had to do with Palestinian widows being appointed to such a ministry while Hellenistic widows were being excluded. The seven, then, who were appointed over this matter did not act as distributors of food to widows, but supervisors of the widows who ministered. While this view might not be well supported among scholars, it is worthy of consideration.

A second reference to widows by Luke concerns a woman named Dorcas.[25] While Peter was preaching in nearby Lydda, word came that this woman had died. The writer is careful to point out that she was much loved, and had abounded in deeds of charity and kindness. It appears that she performed these works as part of a group of widows, since when Peter arrived certain widows were mourning over her body and they showed him the tunics and garments she had made "while she was with them." Had they been the recipients of her charity it is likely that the writer would have said "for them" instead of "with them."

It is also noteworthy that after her resurrection Peter called for the saints and widows to see her alive, which leaves the impression that the widows were a class or group in some way distinct from the rest of the community of believers.

The primary source of information concerning widows in the New Testament period is I Timothy 5:3–16. A substantial portion of this letter deals with church offices, perhaps more appropriately described as roles of service in the church, and Timothy's responsibility in selecting and working with each as a minister and evangelist. At times the specific subjects of Paul's discussion are unclear. For example, at the beginning of chapter five it is impossible to determine the status of the older and younger men and women, whether his terms refer to official roles or simply age groups. In the thirteen verses which follow the apostle carefully identifies and discusses a class of women whose problems, needs and unique opportunities of service comprise a special facet of life in the early church.

Although Paul's treatment of the subject forms a medley of inferences, at least five categories of widows are distinguishable.

Those eligible for financial support from the church Paul calls "real widows." The designation of certain widows as not true widows antedates the Jewish culture by centuries, but was part of their laws from the earliest times. The Hebrew substantive *almanah* often denotes a once-married woman who has no means of financial support, that is, a truly destitute widow, as opposed to one whose husband is dead but who either has means of support from the *ketubbah* or is cared for by children. A "widow with living relatives" or with other revenue needs no financial assistance from the Christian community and therefore should not be thought of as destitute. In this connection Paul makes sure to note that those who are unprepared to care for their own needy relatives — and he specifically means widows — "have denied the faith and are worse than unbelievers" (v. 8). The church as a body should not be burdened with a responsibility which can and should be carried by close family members, in order to have funds to help those who are truly destitute.

Although there is no essential merit in poverty Paul extols the true widows simply because their solitude and indigence demand a deeper faith in God for daily sustenance. A widow who has guaranteed maintenance might well be listed among the idle rich, and is described by Paul as "self-indulgent" and "dead while she lives."

A legitimate need for financial aid could not be determined categorically by age, for no doubt certain young widows with small children, no other living relatives and perhaps no prospects of marrying would be considered destitute. Nor is it feasible that charity would be provided only for widows over the age of sixty, with no consideration for those younger who might be ill, handicapped or burdened with several dependent children. So it would seem that the early church would have considered any widow to be a "real widow" if she had legitimate needs, regardless of age or personal qualities.

Concerning "the young widow" Paul recommends marrying, raising children and keeping a home. In this he sees a noble lifestyle, in keeping with godly principles and social standards of the day. He does not recommend any kind of celibate vow or dedication to an exclusive order which might prove too demanding or unfulfilling for a young woman full of life and passion. Orders of nuns which arose in later centuries often took in young women and demanded a vow of celibacy, quite in opposition to the advice of this apostle.

The primary group of widows discussed by Paul in this section are "enrolled widows." The term *katalegein* means "to place on a list," and suggests an enrollment of widows serving the Lord according to a vow for the rest of their years. This group apparently comprised an honor roll among widows, or widow's guild. There can be no doubt that they were special in that stringent qualifications are set down comparable to those given for elders and deacons in the same letter. The first is that they be no less than sixty years old. Although no reason is given for this particular age, one can assume that widows over sixty would be less likely to remarry or to develop an intimate relationship which might confuse their priorities. It further suggests that enrollment was not simply for the purpose of financial aid.

We do know that sixty was the age chosen by Plato for men and women to join the priesthood in his ideal state,[26] and in the east was considered to be the right age for retirement from the world to quiet contemplation. In the apostolic church, so it would seem, widows of sixty years of age were due some special honor by enrollment in an order from which there would probably be no resignation except in death.

A second requirement for enrollment was that a widow had lived as "the wife of one man." Paul is not inconsistent in his advice about remarriage, though at first this might appear the case. Every widow has the right to remarry, and there is nothing in the New Testament to suggest that such would be slanderous or ignoble.[27] Although Paul preferred the single life and recommended it to both the unmarried and widows, he was aware that natural desires were acceptably satisfied in marriage and that coping with celibacy might be a gift possessed by only a few.[28] It would seem then that a widow who had survived two or three husbands would not be the subject of this contingency. The expression *enos andros gune* carries basically the same meaning for a widow as the expression *mias gunaikos andra* used in reference to elders and deacons, translated "husband of one wife," with probable reference to marriage, divorce and remarriage. Neither is polygamy the issue, for such was not common in the Greco-Roman world nor first-century Judaism and would be denounced by Christian principles in general. Therefore it is reasonable to conclude that Paul had in mind for elders, deacons and enrolled widows marital backgrounds unmarred by divorce and remarriage. Adultery was an enigma of the day, and while there is no evidence of withholding baptism or denying membership to converts with complicated and tainted backgrounds, it is possible that such would eliminate them from special positions of leadership and exemplary service. Lenski aptly interprets the expression used by Paul as "having been true and faithful to one married spouse."[29]

Later on certain church fathers misunderstood this teaching, and seemingly Paul's general attitude toward marriage. The Shepherd of Hermas regarded the remarriage of a widow a horror, and Athenagoras called it a tolerable form of adultery. During their time celibacy was becoming more common as a form of spiritual devotion and marriage was looked upon as mundane and too earthy for anyone truly devoted to God. Paul's celibacy became a model for monastic vows.

Further requirements for enrollment indicate a history of devoted Christian service. The nature of the hospitality for which such a widow must be known indicates her to have been reasonably wealthy. This, coupled with the implication that she now has grown children, would deny the enrolled widow a place among "widows indeed." Therefore, her enrollment is not for financial aid. The same information concerning her background renders it unlikely that she would be appointed to an office in which she would perform the same deeds she has been performing unofficially throughout her Christian life. Authorities in general assume the enrolled widows to have received support from the church, in return for which they cared for orphans, tended the sick, showed hospitality, and gave themselves to spiritual meditation. But neither financial aid nor specific duties can be associated with the enrolled widows on the basis of this passage.

The suggestion of various duties for enrolled widows is not without merit, however. One can see little logic in enrolled widows who now retire and do nothing at a time of their lives in which performing charitable tasks for others would be of significant therapeutic value to themselves. It is clear that their status was of practical value, but not one of administrative authority, even with regard to other women. The fact that younger widows are unsuitable for the position, in that they are likely to become busybodies, "gadding about from house to house" and spreading tales, indicates that the "enrolled widows" would have visitation responsibilities in the homes of other Christians. Their maturity would ensure that they kept to their business and avoided idle chat. Being veterans in every sphere of Christianity, such widows would be ideal teachers for younger women. Perhaps it is in this area that enrolled widows served best.

Paul makes reference to "the older women" in his letter to Titus.[30] The identity of those discussed, like those in I Timothy 5:1–2, is obscure, but the qualities expected of "the older women" and the responsibility to teach younger women "to love their husbands and children, to be sensible, chaste, domestic, kind, and submissive to their husbands" could easily be associated with outstanding women whom Paul calls "enrolled widows."

Widows in Post-Apostolic History

As one might expect, the "order of widows" discussed by Paul becomes much more elaborate in definition and function in post-apostolic history. They are discussed as a special group long before lengthy treatments of deaconesses appear. The first mention of widows by the apostolic fathers is in a much-disputed passage by Ignatius, writing around A.D. 110–117: "I salute the households of my brethren, with their wives and children, and those that are ever virgins, and the widows."[31] Both virgins and widows come to be significant classes of women in the church at a later stage, and at the time of Ignatius it can be accepted that an "order of widows" existed in perhaps every congregation. But Ignatius mentions neither their functions nor the requirements for enrollment.

Polycarp wrote to the Philippians in the early second century:

> Teach the widows to be discreet as respects the faith of the Lord, praying continually for all, being far from all slandering, evil speaking, false witnessing, love of money, and every kind of evil; knowing that they are the altar of God . . .[32]

Justin in his *First Apology*, dated around the middle of the second century, mentioned widows briefly in connection with the Sunday assembly of Christians, stating only that they and orphans were among those assisted out of the funds given each week.[33] No mention is made of an order of widows or a special enrollment. Lucian, also of the middle second century, satirizes Christian practice in his account of the imprisonment of Proteus Peregrinus. Lucian says that Christians:

> . . . left no stone unturned in their endeavor to procure his release. When this proved impossible they looked after his wants in all other matters with untiring solicitude and devotion. From earliest dawn old women (widows) and orphan children might be seen waiting about the prison doors, while the officers of the church, by bribing the jailors, were able to spend the night inside with him. Meals were brought in and they went through their sacred formulas.[34]

From this testimony one might conclude that widows at this stage took responsibility for orphans and that they visited prisoners routinely, perhaps lingering outside in prayer. Although Lucian's work is fiction, it is based on his own observations of Christian behavior and must be regarded as a valid witness.

Tertullian, representing the church in North Africa around A.D. 220, distinctly mentions an order of widows, indicating that they were at least sixty years of age, single-husbanded, mothers, educators of children and counselors to women with problems. He complains that in a certain place a virgin of less than twenty years was placed in the order of widows, much to the detriment of its purpose.[35]

The most comprehensive treatment of widows in post-apostolic history appears in the *Apostolic Constitutions*. In these documents a careful distinction is made between "enrolled widows" and those widows who were merely the recipients of charity. Enrolled widows were expected to spend much time in prayer for the church, and were instructed not to run about from house to house. They were also employed to tend to the sick, instruct the younger women, and to teach Christianity to heathen women.[36]

Distinction Between Widows and Deaconesses

Evidence leaves little doubt about the existence of some kind of order of widows in the apostolic church. The requirements for enrollment, the nature of duties, and the distinction between "enrolled widows" and "widows indeed" appear to have remained fairly constant from New Testament times down to the fifth century, which was not the case with deaconesses. It also appears that eventually the two became blended in the east and deaconesses replaced widows altogether in the west till both were abolished.

At the time of the *Apostolic Constitutions*, third and fourth centuries, confusion was being felt about the two orders. Deaconesses were almost thought of as church officers being appointed by the imposition of hands, but widows not. They were distinct groups, with widows subject to the authority of deaconesses. But the same collection of documents requires a deaconess to be either a pure virgin or a widow who has been married once.[37] The Council of Nicea, dated A.D. 325, speaks only of deaconesses as a recognized female order in the church. The Council of Orleans, around A.D. 533, speaks of "widows who are called deaconesses." Concerning the two orders Lightfoot says: "Whatever confusion there may have been in later times, in the apostolic age and for some generations after Ignatius they were distinct."[38]

III. VIRGINS

The Roman Catholic Church claims that its various orders of nuns date from the earliest days of the church, but in truth they arose out of and in replacement of the deaconesses and enrolled widows, with the vows of perpetual chastity adopted from the primitive orders of virgins. But of the three, the latter finds the least support in the New Testament in terms of a formal order or office.

Two groups of virgins are mentioned in the New Testament as pertaining to the church. Luke states that Philip the Evangelist had "four virgin daughters who prophesied," and Paul in his first letter to the Corinthians discusses virgins in the context of problems surroundng marriage in times of stress.[39] The daughters of Philip are of significance because of their gifts of prophecy and will be discussed under another heading. But in neither of the passages is there any reason to believe that a special order of virgins existed in the apostolic church, much less an official status of leadership. There were those in Paul's time who forbade marriage, but their doctrine was regarded as heretical. Some may have chosen a celibate life for personal reasons, but there is no indication in the New Testament that such a vow had any spiritual value, either for the individual or for the church.

Very early in the second century the practice of abstaining from marriage became common among Christians.[40] Justin refers to many men and women of the age of seventy who had kept themselves unpolluted sexually.[41] The salute to virgins at Smyrna by Ignatius, already cited, is noteworthy.[42] Tertullian probably writes more concerning the demeanor of virgins in the church than any other patristic writer.[43] But nothing concerning an "order of virgins," implying a special class of women with a vow to perpetual virginity, can be found earlier than the *Apostolic Constitutions.* Here virgins are listed with deaconesses and widows as worthy of special honor. Virgins are commanded to refrain from running from house to house spreading stories, and are advised rather to do such things as are suitable to the vow.[44] Virgins, like widows, were not ordained, but were regarded as engaging in a state of voluntary trial. There is evidence that as early as the third century community houses had been established where these women could live in seclusion, and about that time they came to be accepted as a special class in the church. The first convent was established by Pachomius in the early fourth century.

Nevertheless, a treatment of I Corinthians 7 is necessary since this chapter provides access to the mind of Paul on the subjects of celibacy and virginity, and since it is quite clear that later related church orders have their roots here and perhaps in Jesus' statement concerning eunuchs for the kingdom's sake, even if they did not exist in the apostolic period. The chapter is divided naturally into the following five sections.

Celibacy, Verses 1–7

The essence of Paul's teaching here is that celibacy is good, but marriage is natural. It is clear from verse 1 that the Corinthians had raised this question in a letter to Paul, and in response Paul states his preference. Not so clear is whether Paul thought of continence as a concession or marriage as a concession, but he does suggest that the ability to contain is as much a gift of God as marriage.[45]

Paul's directives on celibacy can only be understood in light of his feeling that for those who possess the gift of continence the celibate life, for religious purposes, represents a higher plane and a greater degree of dedication to the Lord than the married life. This attitude in Paul is quite heterogenous to genuine Judaism.[46] But the apostle recognizes that the weakness and inclinations of the flesh render this life impractical for the average Christian. Marriage is far more noble than a celibate life under strain of temptation. Therefore for those who have married Paul allows abstinence for short periods for prayer and fasting, but only by mutual consent. He emphasizes the obligation of both husband and wife to render conjugal rights, so that neither partner suffers temptation to immorality.

Unmarried and Widows, Verses 8–9

The writer then focuses attention briefly on bachelors, widowers and widows. For the first time in the chapter Paul speaks of absolute celibacy, which he describes as good, suggesting the acceptability of this pattern of life if the individual is so inclined. Some understand his phrase "even as I" to indicate that Paul was a widower. It seems that membership in the Sanhedrin required a man to be married with children. But whether Paul was a part of this Jewish council is a matter of speculation, and therefore it is impossible to know whether he had ever been married. Nonetheless, encouragement to follow a celibate lifestyle is negated if an individual does not have the power of continence. For such men and women, says Paul, it is far better to marry rather than attempt a single life while burning with passion. Similar advice is given by Paul to younger widows in I Timothy 5:11–15.

Pauline Privilege, Verses 10–16

This section contains advice to those already married. Verses 10–11, which introduce this portion of the material, appear to speak primarily to those who are married to Christians, and represent Paul's endorsement of Jesus' teaching concerning marriage and divorce. Divorce is prohibited, whether initiated by the wife or by the husband. Paul adds, to cover the possibility that some of the Corinthians had already done so, that if a wife does leave her husband she should either seek reconciliation or remain single. The same advice would apply to a husband who had divorced his wife.

The remainder of this section pertains to mixed marriages, that is, marriages between a Christian and a non–Christian. We must assume that such marriages had become unpleasant due to the incompatibility of Christianity and pagan religions, and the question no doubt arose as to whether a Christian had the right to divorce his (or her) partner when the latter refused to abjure paganism. Paul points out a necessary distinction at this point. If the unbelieving partner is content with the present state of things divorce is not only unnecessary but forbidden. In fact, the maintenance of such a marriage can serve for the positive influence of both the unbelieving partner and their children.

It appears that some converts tried to use the incompatibility of their faith with paganism as an excuse to put away unbelieving partners. Perhaps some of the Jewish sector appealed to the case of foreign wives being dismissed at the command of Ezra during the restoration period. But there is little reason to think that such a marriage is any less valid than any other. The union is pure and lawful. But if the unbelieving partner is not content and desires a divorce the Christian is not compelled to sacrifice his faith in order to preserve the marriage. In such a case, Paul says, the brother or sister "is not bound." It is incorrect to argue that Paul here grants concession to divorce or that he implies the liberty of the repudiated Christian partner to remarry. The only "Pauline privilege" is that a brother or sister need not feel so bound by Christ's prohibition of divorce as to be afraid to depart when the pagan partner insists on separation. The right of remarriage is here a moot issue.

The Life Which the Lord Has Assigned, Verses 17–24

The next section begins awkwardly with "do not be," suggesting a conditional clause which does not appear here. Paul no doubt alludes to the possibility implied in the preceding two questions. But the apodosis is unclear, since he offers in the remainder of the sentence advice which grammatically should be an alternative, and is in fact the same course of action suggested in verses 10–16; namely, to seek to remain in whatever state one was called. The appeal to circumcision and slavery is clearly illustrative, the writer's objective being to persuade each Christian to remain in whatever marital state he may have been upon conversion to Christianity. Such advice is certainly in harmony with Paul's respect for the matrimonial bond, but at the same time strongly emphasizes his own personal preference.

Virgins, Verses 25–40

The last section of the chapter is the longest, and the most problematic. Those concerning whom Paul speaks are identified as virgins (*parthenoi*). Perhaps it is this very term which gives rise to interpretive difficulties, for a number of contrasting explanations of the pericope have been suggested by scholars, and the meaning of *parthenos* is consistently the point of divergence.

J. Massyngberde Ford, for example, argues that the word "virgin" in Hebrew, Greek and Latin does not always refer to a woman or man who has never been married (i.e. never experienced coitus), but rather that it is a term of status; one who has been married only once, and who is pure by merit of faithfulness to one partner. On this basis she approaches I Corinthians 7:25–40, suggesting that Paul here refers to young widows and widowers, rather than virgins, and that the subject under discussion is Levirate marriage.[47] This theory, though interesting, is unacceptable in that it makes far too much of an obscure and questionable use of *parthenos* and because it presupposes the practice of Jewish Levirate marriage among Corinthian Christians, most of whom were of pagan background.

In contrast, J.K. Elliott understands *parthenos* to mean "betrothed girl," and argues that the entire passage deals with engaged couples. But Elliott's translation of *qune* as "woman" (which he takes to suggest fiancee) rather than "wife" (v. 27), *luein* as "to break off an engagement" rather than "to divorce" (v. 27), and *gamidzein* as "to marry" rather than the usual "to give in marriage," tend to render his approach rather tenuous.[48]

A closer look at the passage reveals that *parthenos* is best understood in its basic sense of "virgin," and that verses 25–38 are predominantly concerned with the marriage of virgins. On this subject no traditional teaching of Jesus had reached the apostle, and it appears that he had received no special revelation on it. Therefore, he offers his own opinion determined by what he terms "the present necessity."

Paul's feelings about remaining single were determined largely by the difficult times in which he lived, combined with a more intense expectation of the end of the world than is felt by most believers today. Under these circumstances this dedicated apostle felt that freedom to be devoted totally to the service of the Lord, without encumbrance or distraction, was preferable. With this in mind verses 32 and 35 draw together both virgins and those who might have been married at one stage in their lives but are now single, declaring the benefit of their freedom to commit themselves to God.

This overall context provides the groundwork for an understanding of verses 27–28, which come before Paul's mention of critical times. His earlier rejection of divorce is reiterated, using the term *lusis*, which appears only here in all the New Testament. The same rejection is apparent in his advice, "If you are loosed from a wife do not seek a wife." The added warning in verse 28 implies that a wrong decision will likely result in bitterness and regret later, but there is nothing to suggest that such a marriage is regarded as sinful. Paul is speaking of practicality here, not morality.

The approach taken in studying this section of scripture by many commentators seems to hinge upon the same questions asked of Jesus by Jewish scholars concerning grounds for divorce and remarriage. Some churchmen are obsessed with determining the morality of relationships, not from the standpoint of a couple's own conscience but for the benefit of others who find themselves in the dubious position of guarding the doors of God's kingdom. To their thinking, Jesus quite clearly taught that marriage after an unacceptable divorce constitutes adultery, and if Paul here allows remarriage there arises a contradiction between his doctrine and that of Christ. Since that cannot be allowed, Paul must be saying something else.

To alleviate the tension some scholars have understood *lelusai* to mean simply "unattached," in no way suggesting divorce and referring only to bachelors, virgins and widows. But it may be that all alleged disharmony arises from drawing far too much from Jesus' teaching, since the thrust of all his statements on divorce was to denounce the evil motives behind it and since most church dogma on this question is founded upon debatable inferences and assumptions rather than fact.

Verse 36 must be understood in light of the *patria potestas*, a concept which was quite the norm in Paul's day and which was discussed earlier in this text in connection with Roman women. At this point in the epistle Paul's advice turns to fathers who may have had reservations about allowing their daughters to marry, considering the troubled times and imminent persecution. Yet the language indicates that both fathers and family might feel it unfair to refuse permission, especially if a daughter was past her prime marriageable age, which Plato fixed at twenty.[49] The father is justified in exercising his paternal right, Paul says, using his best judgment in deciding whether to let her marry or to keep her a virgin.

The last advice in this section concerns widows only. Paul presents a similar axiom in Romans 7:1–6 to illustrate the transition from law to grace in Christ, but here he applies it in its natural sense to marriage. A widow has the right to remarry, provided she marries a believer ("in the Lord"). This is quite harmonious with I Timothy 5:14, but as in all other cases Paul seems confident that a widow will be happier if she remains single.

4. Female Leadership in the Early Christian Assembly

The participation of women in the formal assembly of the early church, along with their involvement in preaching, is probably a more controversial issue in the church today than is the possibility of female officers. It is relatively certain that women had a part in proclaiming the Gospel to non-believers at least during the period in which charismatic gifts were operative. Apart from teaching by inspiration, most of the activities of women in instructing other Christians seem to be outside the assembly. But evidence is strong that women participated in singing and prayers when Christians came together, and could engage in open discussions with the speaker. Activities which might be considered leadership in these proceedings were limited but are identifiable under three headings: prophecy, teaching and praying.

I. PROPHETESSES

In order to comprehend the function of prophetesses in the early Christian community it will be necessary first to examine the concept of prophecy, in both the Old and New Testaments.

Old Testament Prophecy

In the Old Testament the term designating a prophet is *nabi'*, which occurs over three hundred times in the masculine form, and six times with a feminine suffix. The root meaning is "to utter a sound" or "to announce, speak, or proclaim," and is thought to relate to the term *naba'*, meaning "to bubble, or pour forth like a spring."[1] A synonymous term is *rueh*, meaning "a seer," who sees and hears things not within the scope of natural perception. Prophetism in cultures antedating that of Israel and in some of its

76

contemporary cultures was marked by frenzy and ecstatic speech. It was believed that a seer, as most ethnic prophets were known, might be seized suddenly by a spirit causing him to rave as if possessed, and in this state to utter messages from the world beyond.[2] Most of the prophetic practices in Egypt, Babylon, Assyria, Canaan and other ancient cultures are related primarily to magic and astrology, and the ecstatic experiences and dreams were, for the most part, induced by artificial means such as drugs or hypnotic trance.

The Egyptian envoy Wen-Amon (around 1100 B.C.) is reported to have witnessed a young prophet in Phoenicia who had a frenzy while seized by one of his gods, and the ancient Babylonians and Assyrians are said to have had prophets "possessed" by their god, who caused them to act in an irrational and uncontrolled manner.

Old Testament prophets also were involved to a certain extent with visions, dreams and forecasts, and were characterized by strange behavior. But as a whole they represent a very practical type of ministry, including social, religious and political reform.

Essentially, the prophet of Yahweh was a proclaimer of religious truth and of the profound mysteries of the kingdom of God. He was the mouthpiece of God driven by his zeal and by the burden of a divinely inspired message to preach to God's people. We have little reason to view him as ecstatic or as an automaton under the slavish control of God. His own personality was constantly evident, and he was in total control of his behavior. Prediction of the future was not the principal element in Old Testament prophecy. Prediction was certainly employed by most, and the fulfillment of their prophecies served as evidence of divine calling. But the Old Testament "man of God" was primarily a man of the present. He interpreted the meaning of military defeats, grasshopper plagues and famines to the immediate spiritual needs of the people. He predicted the future and recalled the past for the purpose of motivation toward allegience to God.

Although men dominate the prophetic office in the Old Testament, it would seem that women were not categorically excluded. The term "prophetess" is applied to Miriam, the sister of Moses; to Deborah, one of the judges prior to the monarchy; to Huldah, a contemporary of Jeremiah and apparently a functioning female prophet; to Noadiah, a professional prophetess who opposed the work of Nehemiah; and to the wife of Isaiah.[3] In the Gospels the term *prophetis* is applied to Anna, who is doubtless a remnant of the Old Testament prophetic ministry.[4]

New Testament Prophecy

The verb for prophesying in the New Testament Greek is *propheteuein* and the noun for the prophet is *prophetes*. The use of these terms in the Septuagint shows them to be the equivalent of *nabi'* and its root verb. The masculine *prophetes* is found one hundred and forty nine times in the New Testament, with the feminine *prophetis* occurring twice. In Classical Greek a prophet was an interpreter or expounder of the will of the gods to man. In the New Testament the noun is used to describe the prophets of the Old Testament, and is applied to John the Baptist and Jesus as spokesmen for God. But of primary significance is the application of the same ancient term to the prophet of the New Testament church. It is here that the term *prophetes* has its clearest definition. Lexicographers seem to agree that the prophet in the early church was not a seer of visions nor a prophet of future events, but an inspired preacher or teacher and an organ of special revelation from God, functioning under the guidance of the Holy Spirit. He was a proclaimer of the word of God, and his calling was not to "foretell" but to "forth tell." Some aspects of the prophecies uttered by this kind of prophet may have been apocalyptic in nature, but for the most part the message was straightforward and quite relevant to the lives of the prophet's audience.

Several significant factors characterized New Testament prophecy:

1. The primary purpose was to bear witness to Jesus Christ and to edify the Christian assembly.

2. The office, or ministry, of the prophet appears to have been associated with one of the charismatic gifts imparted by the laying on of apostolic hands. Friedrich states that "primitive Christian prophecy is the inspired speech of charismatic preachers. . . ."[5]

3. Utterances of Christian prophets were intelligible to both the audience and the prophet himself.[6]

4. The prophet had the responsibility to use his ability while properly keeping his own motives and life in check.

5. The spirits of prophecy and tonguespeaking were not ecstatic, but were in the control of the prophet. He was not beside himself but was in complete control of his gift and in contact with reality.

6. The assembly, perhaps with the aid of someone gifted with discernment of spirits, was to determine whether a prophecy was genuinely inspired.[7]

7. Paul regarded the gift of prophecy to be the highest and most profitable of all charismatic gifts, placing the prophet next to the apostles in significance to the foundation of the church.[8]

8. Prophets, like the apostles, were not church officers but the agents of God in a special ministry.[9]

9. Prophecy after this fashion, along with other charismatic gifts, was transient in nature, destined to disappear when its purpose in the infancy of the church had been served.[10]

Therefore it can be said with reasonable certainty that prophets in the apostolic church were essentially inspired preachers of the will of God, serving primarily for the edification of the Christian community. They were not merely recognized as prophets because of repeated utterances in assembly, but rather were known in their own community as those who had been endowed with the gift of prophecy and who were a living testimony to the validity of the Christian message.

Nature of the Early Christian Assembly

A number of passages give the impression that prophets had almost unlimited freedom of utterance in the assemblies of the apostolic church.[11] Each contributed, according to his *charisma*, to a common stock of divinely revealed information. To this fact Paul alluded in his statement, "We know in part and prophesy in part."[12] Thus the congregation learned the doctrines and principles of the New Covenant by piecing together the revelations of various charismatic prophets, and this piecing was verified by the apostles and by those possessing other charismatic gifts such as interpretation of tongues, wisdom, discerning of spirits and so on.

The thought of numerous prophets speaking at will seems puzzling until one considers that the format of the early church gatherings differed greatly from most of those of the twentieth century. Customarily, the "sermon" was conducted more in the form of a discussion, with questions and responses from the audience, and frequently there were several principal speakers. These facts are indicated primarily by the terminology used by New Testament writers to describe preaching the word of God to an audience of believers, and a brief discussion of such terms will be helpful at this point in order to elucidate the part played by prophets.

A term which is found repeatedly throughout Acts is *dialegesthai*, meaning "to hold a dialogue with."[13] This word describes the speech made by Paul at Troas on the first day of the week which, according to Acts 10:7f., lasted till midnight. The same term is used whenever Paul, according to his custom on the Sabbath, discussed portions of the Old Testament scriptures in the synagogue. The synagogue format centered around reading the Law and prayer, but comments and speeches were made by anyone who may have been recognized as having the knowledge and talent to do so. It was on such an occasion that Paul was invited to address the synagogue gathering in Antioch of Pisidia, following the reading of the Law and the Prophets. The speaker stood before the group, and during his presentation could be interrupted with questions or responses from the floor. It was upon this format that the Christian assembly was based.

Another significant term in this context is *homilein*, which means "to discuss" or "to converse." This is the word which describes the continuation

of Paul's speech till dawn, following the fall of Eutychus from the third loft
(Acts 20:11). The same term is employed throughout the New Testament
to describe a conversation between two people or more,[14] and became the
favorite technical expression in the post-apostolic period for delivering a
sermon. It is so used by Ignatius in his letter to Polycarp, and by Justin in
his dialogue with Trypho.[15] In both cases the original idea of an exchange
of thoughts, particularly with regard to scripture, is till retained.

This type of teaching through dialogue was employed by Jesus and is
described by the term *didaskein* in the Gospels.[16] The same concept came
into the writings of Paul as "doctrine," which appears to be closely
associated with mutual admonition within the church.[17] The stability of the
early Christian community depended upon the mutual responsibility of its
members to participate in reciprocal admonition in the form of songs,
prayers and teaching.[18] This was the purpose of the assembly.[19] And in this
context the New Testament prophets saw the fulfillment of their own purpose and ministry.

The Role of Prophetesses

During the Pentecost sermon (Acts 2) Peter quoted the prophetic
words of Joel:

> And it shall be in the last days, God says, that I will pour forth my
> spirit upon all mankind; and your sons and your daughters shall proph-
> esy, and your young men shall see visions, and your old men shall dream
> dreams; even upon my bondslaves, both men and women, I will in those
> days pour forth of my spirit and they shall prophesy.[20]

In view of the apocalyptic nature of this prophecy it is difficult to determine
to what extent this portion of the text can be taken literally. It does appear
that some type of ministry by inspired women was to be a sign of the
presence of the Holy Spirit and the initiation of a new age for God's people.
But there is considerable disagreement as to when it may have begun. The
majority of scholars hold that the one hundred and twenty disciples of the
previous chapter were assembled on this occasion and that the entire group
received the "outpouring" of the Holy Spirit, evidenced by tongues of fire
and the ability to speak in other languages. If this is the case, then of
necessity a number of women were endowed with the gift of tongues at the
outset of the church, for Luke mentions "the women and Mary the mother
of Jesus" as among the company of disciples.

There is the possibility, however, that only the apostles received the
miraculous evidences of the Spirit. The latter view is more harmonious

with other evidence in Acts, and does no harm to the prophecy. The words of Joel are apparently fulfilled over a period of time, rather than at a single event. Therefore, if inspired prophetesses appeared anywhere during the early stages of the church, this would be understood as a sign of the new age and the fulfillment of prophecy.

The first clear mention of female prophetism in the history of the early church is the case of the four daughters of Philip. These were single girls, described as virgins, whose father was one of the seven chosen in Jerusalem and who had become known for his evangelism and miraculous gifts of the Spirit.[21] They were present when the prophet Agabus warned Paul of the dangers which awaited him in Jerusalem. By the time these events transpired, prophetic gifts had long been in use in Corinth, and Paul had already written a letter dealing extensively with the misuse of charismatic abilities in that church. It could be argued that Philip's daughters and Agabus were remnants of Old Testament prophetism, as probably was Anna, or that they were called to some special prophetic ministry such as that of John the Baptist. But evidence concerning New Testament prophecy in general makes it reasonably certain that the daughters of Philip had received the imposition of apostolic hands and were now functioning in the church as inspired proclaimers of the word of God. And the general tone of I Corinthians 14 is that such prophets spoke primarily for the edification of the Christian assembly.

Of considerable importance to the discussion of prophetesses is Paul's first letter to the Corinthians. Commentators wrestle with what appears to be a blatant contradiction in policy, in that Paul in one chapter acknowledges the ministry of prophetesses and in another chapter seems to deny them the right to speak. The apparent injunction of silence in I Corinthians 14 will be discussed later, and an effort will be made to reconcile the two passages. At this point it will suffice to ascertain whether prophetesses existed in Corinth, and whether or not they exercised their gift in the assembly. Paul states:

> Any man who prays or prophesies with his head covered dishonors his head, but any woman who prays or prophesies with her head uncovered dishonors her head . . .[22]

It can be said with reasonable certainty that those women to whom Paul refers were inspired prophetesses, and were preaching in some formal manner. This fact is far better attested by biblical writers than is the office of deaconess, and Paul's manner of expression leaves little alternative interpretation. Irenaeus, writing around A.D. 185, so understood the passage: "For in his (Paul's) Epistle to the Corinthians, he speaks expressly of prophetical gifts, and recognizes men and women prophesying in the church."[23]

In the middle second century a movement began in Phrygia, led by one Montanus, to purify the church by returning to the principles of the primitive community and by reviving prophetic gifts. Among the Montanists, as they became known, were two outstanding women named Maximilla and Priscilla. The movement was condemned as heretical by the orthodox church, and eventually disappeared entirely. The claimed restoration of prophetic gifts is recognized by authorities as ecstatic utterances rather than divine inspiration, although many scholars feel that the gifts associated with the first century church were really no more than ecstatic utterances also. But the testimony of Montanism adds to the evidence that prophetesses did exist in the apostolic church. Tertullian represents the Montanist interpretation of Paul's reference:

> . . . when enjoining on a woman silence in the church that they speak not for the mere sake of learning (although that even they have the right of prophesying, he has already shown when he covers the woman that prophesies with a veil), he goes to the law for this sanction that women should be under obedience.[24]

Although the patristic writers are often unreliable as exegetes, or as witnesses to the status quo in the apostolic period, there does appear merit in their unanimous recognition of the existence of prophetesses in the early church. Of considerable importance also is the agreement among the fathers that the miraculous gifts described by Paul in I Corinthians had ceased by their own time, indicating that the ministry of prophets and prophetesses was limited to the apostolic age. With reference to the gifts of the Spirit, John Chrysostom admitted:

> This whole place is very obscure: but the obscurity is produced by our ignorance of the facts referred to and by their cessation, being such as then used to occur but now no longer take place.[25]

A question remains as to when and where prophetesses may have engaged in their inspired ministry. Concerning I Corinthians 11:5, the most widely held opinion is that Paul is referring to the exercise of prophetic gifts in the general assembly of the church based upon three very obvious factors:

1. It appears that the entire section 11:2–14:34 deals with matters concerning the assembly.

2. The nature of the gift of prophecy implies its use when the entire congregation is assembled together.

3. The relation of the use of prophecy to "head covering" implies some standard of propriety for appearance before a gathering.

But there are those who find it difficult to accept that women could have exercised such leadership before an assembled body of Christians, and several alternative theories have been suggested.

Bachmann and a few others have argued that prophetesses were permitted to speak on occasions of private home devotions, defined as assemblies of limited circles such as "house-churches," or perhaps even at family devotionals.[26] One of the arguments used to support this theory is that 8:1–11:1 should be seen as a unit dealing with domestic problems, and the change to congregational meetings is made only in 11:7 at the beginning of the Lord's Supper discussion. This would mean that the verse in question was intended to be understood as part of a household problem, perhaps that of respect for the husband's authority. Admittedly, points of transition in Pauline material are always somewhat indistinct, and one topic might flow into another through associated concepts or terminology. But in I Corinthians 11 the clear relationship of the first section to the Lord's Supper discussion which follows cannot be ignored in favor of the above theory.

Another point which might be raised in favor of domestic devotionals is the implication that only married prophetesses are involved in the problem at hand, since the discussion revolves around husband-wife relationships. The failure to mention single girls suggests to some scholars that whatever difficulties existed were restricted to the home, and that the gatherings must have been of a private nature. On the contrary, what is suggested is that the most significant problem created by the miraculous prophetic ministry of women was in the realm of husband-wife relationships, with repercussions even in the church assembly.

Very similar to the above argument is the suggestion by Prohl that the agape (love feast) and the eucharist (Lord's Supper) were closed feasts, to which only the initiated were invited.[27] He asserts that where no outsiders were present the wives were permitted to join the men in leading prayers and in prophesying. However, there is no suggestion in the New Testament that non-believers were prohibited from attending any of the assemblies, and I Corinthians 14 implies quite the opposite, that unbelievers were welcome. It seems that secret or closed meetings only arose out of necessity during the periods of extreme persecution, and as long as the Christians were in no physical danger their assemblies were open to any passerby. The theories of private devotionals and closed meetings as solutions to the problem of female prophetism are rejected by most scholars today.

Other theories to be rejected include that of Robertson and Plummer, who suggest that Paul simply made allowance in I Corinthians 11 for a hypothetical, and unlikely, occasion of a woman being moved by the Spirit to speak, in which case she should be veiled.[28]

A more acceptable alternative is that Paul's concern was for the decorum of men and women exercising prophetic gifts in public places, and for their compliance with social norms. This line of reasoning presupposes the responsibility of Christians to conduct themselves before the public eye without offense or cause for accusation. Assuming that headcoverings were required of women appearing in public, or perhaps of women participating in some type of religious observance, one might conclude that the need for Christian prophetesses to conform to certain customs emerged out of social propriety. Prophecy did occur outside the assembly, and it is noteworthy that the daughters of Philip who were recognized for their prophetic abilities were present when Agabus delivered his prophetic warning to Paul.[29] Although prophecy was used in the assembly to benefit the entire church, its effectiveness was not limited to that occasion. In fact, I Corinthians 14:6 implies that a prophet might also possess the gift of tonguespeaking, or that a tonguespeaker might teach by prophecy, and therefore would have the capacity to participate in public evangelism.

It is known that at the establishment of the church preaching occurred in many public places, such as the temple grounds and porches, synagogues, market places (*agora*), and along city streets. The earliest congregations gathered in such public places as well as in private homes, at least until their stability and organization permitted their procuring permanent meeting places. Therefore, it would be reasonable to assume that the conduct of Christians when assembled would be witnessed almost constantly by non-believers. The church at Corinth, by the time Paul wrote the two known epistles to that group, was quite large and had developed a customary order of proceedings for its regular assembly. The language of I Corinthians 14 strongly suggests a formal assembly into which visitors might come, rather than a disorganized crowd gathered in full public view.

Therefore, it is necessary to conclude that the proceedings implied by the term "prophesying" in I Corinthians 11:5 were involved with the assembly of the church, and that women who possessed prophetic gifts played an active role in inspired teaching and preaching, both in assemblies and in public evangelism.

One need not look for special references to prophetesses once it is established that they existed, for the masculine plural would doubtless include all females with the same prophetic gift. But, to add to the evidence already noted, there is one other New Testament reference to a prophetess. In Revelation 2:20 the apostle, John, or whoever may be credited with the work, rebukes the church at Thyatira in the following terms:

> But I have this against you, that you tolerate the woman Jezebel, who calls herself a prophetess, and she teaches and leads My bond-servants astray, so that they commit acts of immorality and eat things sacrificed to idols.

Some authorities regard the woman to have been a real figure in the church at Thyatira who gained prominence through her charismatic gifts. Caird thinks that since the charge against her so closely resembles that against the Nicolaitans of Pergamum, she may have been a leader of that movement in Thyatira.[30] But in view of the character of The Revelation as a whole, even that of the letters to the seven churches of which this reference is a part, it is likely that the name Jezebel symbolizes false teachers who lead members of the church into idolatry and doctrinal heresy. The name Jezebel, that of the immoral and idolatrous queen of the Old Testament, is used by the writer in much the same way as Jude employed the names of Balaam, Cain and Koreh to typify those who abandon the doctrine of Jesus Christ in favor of emperor worship, Gnosticism, or any other heresy. Nonetheless, the reference tacitly presupposes that women could be, and some actually were, prophetesses in the apostolic church.

II. LEADERS IN PRAYER

The same statement by Paul which indicates that women engaged in prophecy in the assemblies of the Corinthian church also indicates female leadership in public prayer. The term translated "praying" in this passage is used more than eighty times in the New Testament with the same meaning.

Nature of Prayer in the Early Church

A variety of prayer forms came into Christianity from Judaism, such as petitions, supplications, praise, thanksgiving, and such like. But as early as the teachings of Jesus there occurs a shift to a more personal style of prayer which no doubt motivated the disciples, who were accustomed to regular prayer since childhood, to say "Lord teach us to pray."[31] Even in Judaism just prior to the life of Christ prayer came to take the place of sacrifice in a shift of religious emphasis from the nation to the individual. Nash writes that "the immense outflow of spiritual power and moral energy that founded the Christian church made prayer its spring and soul."[32]

New Testament examples and instruction concerning prayer reveal a surprising lack of liturgy, although psalms and devotional forms were incorporated into the wording of many prayers. Prayers appear to have been generally spontaneous and related to special needs and circumstances.

A common attitude of prayer was to hold the arms out with palms open and turned upward, either indicating a request for sustenance, unconditional surrender to God, or even moral purity.[33] But there is no indication that any special attitude was practiced ritually, for New Testament writers as a whole regard virtually any position as acceptable. Early converts seem to be accustomed to keeping hours of prayer, but this may have passed away as the church drifted away from Judaism.

Paul stresses the importance of congregational prayers, often soliciting prayers on behalf of himself and others whose circumstances were precarious. As to whether prayers were recited in unison or worded by an individual nothing concrete can be determined, although scant references, including those to be discussed next, indicate the latter.

The relationship between prayer and inspired prophecy is obscure. Prayer is never listed among charismatic gifts, although some suggest that the prayer to which the Corinthian church would have responded "amen" was worded by a prophet.

Concerning the women who "pray and prophesy" in I Corinthians 11 it is difficult to know whether their prayers were charismatic or by any prophetic authority. But it is likely that those who possessed prophetic abilities were devoted to extensive prayer, and were called upon most often to word prayers for edification when the whole church was together. There is some indication that those in the New Testament who possessed prophetic abilities were given to considerable prayer and meditation.[34]

A second Pauline text which might indicate the participation of women as leaders in public prayer is I Timothy 2:8–10:

> Therefore I want the men in every place to pray, lifting up holy hands, without wrath and dissension. Likewise, I want women to adorn themselves with proper clothing, modestly and discreetly, not with braided hair and gold or pearls or costly garments; but rather by means of good works, as befits women making a claim to godliness.

Paul alludes here to public prayer, the expression "every place" referring to wherever Christians might assemble. But the overall tone of his statement has application in every sphere of Christian life, and not just to a formal assembly. There are some who hold that men only did the praying, and that women in the assembly prayed only after the fashion of Hanna, who spoke in her heart; only her lips moved, but her voice was not heard.[35] There are other authorities, however, who contend that the use of "likewise" connects verse nine with the subject of prayer in the previous eight verses. John Chrysostom, writing late in the fourth century, held this view:

> In like manner, he (Paul) says, "I will that women approach God without wrath and doubting, lifting up holy hands . . ." Paul however requires something more of women, that they adorn themselves "in modest apparel, with shamefacedness and sobriety . . ."[36]

Ramsay contends that "likewise" in this place is meaningless if it does not relate praying to women also, and Lock says that the Greek conjunction may even carry on to women all that has been said concerning men in the previous verses.[37] If this is the case, then the regulations concerning dress in verses nine and ten must be taken to represent the standards expected of those women who play a leading role in the assembly of the church. Much the same principle appears in I Corinthians 11:5 and 13.

Special dress codes for assembly in the first century might have historical support. But if so such would be inconsistent with the non-discriminatory character of Christianity and would also be irrelevant in the modern west.

Comparative silence among patristic writers on the subject of women praying publicly would suggest that phenomena like the ministry of prophetesses had become a thing of the past. Since church history subsequent to the apostolic age reveals a tendency to develop and to exaggerate simple orders, offices and functions, the silence concerning women at prayer would indicate that even in the early church it was a special function which died out soon after the close of the first century. A similar fate having befallen the ministry of prophetesses, noted along with the association of "prayer and prophecy" in various New Testament references, one would conclude that those women who participated in public prayer did so because of their special function as prophetesses. If the purpose for these roles in the early church was to set a precedent for the future, it failed to attain fruition.

III. TEACHERS

The Concept of Teaching

A number of terms appear in the Old Testament which describe the process of imparting wisdom or knowledge, called teaching. In the Jewish home the teaching of the Law was primarily the responsibility of the parents, but provision was made also for public instruction. It seems that generally the ancient teaching process involved lecturing, using poetry, proverbs and historical narrative, while the pupils listened and memorized the oral instruction verbatim.

The Greek term *didaskein* appears as early as the writings of Homer with the simple meaning "to impart knowledge," but very rarely is used in connection with religious instruction. In the Septuagint the same word translates several Hebrew terms and carries both a secular and religious significance. But according to Rengstorf the term increasingly comes to have a technical significance for the Greek-speaking Jews. Both the Hebrew and Greek, he says, denote:

> ... the manner in which, by exposition of the Law as the sum of the
> revealed will of God, instruction is given for the ordering of the relation-
> ship between the individual and God on the one side, and the neighbor
> on the other, according to divine will.[38]

There is a clear relationship between the sage of the ancient world in general
and the teacher in post-exilic Judaism who expounds the law. The latter
replaced the sage in Israel when oral wisdom took a literary form.

The Teaching of Jesus

The Gospels identify teaching as one of the most prominent aspects of
Jesus' public ministry. He seems to have commenced his work in Galilee by
teaching in the synagogues, which were the acknowledged place of instruction.[39] At the synagogue in Nazareth he adopted the format customary
among rabbis of that period. After reading a portion of scripture while
standing, he took a seat and gave an expository lesson from the text he had
read.[40] In other cases he exposed the Torah.[41] For this reason he is identified
as "Rabbi."

In addition it should be noted that a good deal of the Gospel material
generally regarded as sermonic is in fact a compilation of didactic
discourses of Jesus. This is indicated by the various questions which
prompted the discourses, and the frequent interruptions by his audience.
The style Jesus employed seems to have been similar to that of the Greek
diatribe, and therefore should naturally be termed "teaching" rather than
"preaching."

The significance of teaching to Jesus, with regard to the propagation
of the Gospel, is indicated by his last instructions to the apostles before his
ascension. This was to be the principal means by which all nations could
be taught to observe the doctrine of Christ. By this command the early
church received a commission both to proclaim the Gospel and to further
instruct the members of the church. In Matthew 28:19 the term translated
"teach" in the Authorized Version is actually *matheteusate*, the verb form
of "disciple." The process of discipling, or making disciples, followed very
much the pattern to be observed in Jesus' training of his own disciples, that
being an extensive period of close fellowship. This approach was common
among the Greek philosophers.

Nature of Teaching in the Church

A variety of terms are employed by New Testament writers to describe
religious instruction, the process of imparting knowledge in a formal situation. Most of these terms relate to preaching, and have been so translated,

although there are certain distinctions among them. The verb *kerussein*, for example, is used primarily with regard to the proclamation of the good news. Its basic meaning is "to herald," but it cannot correctly be used for the delivery of a learned and edifying hortatory discourse the way it might be thought of today.[42] The terms *homilein, diermeneuein* and *dialegesthai* might be more closely linked with the delivery of a sermon in a formal assembly, but each of these terms carries a precise meaning which expresses the manner of presentation, and none is the equivalent of the western concept of giving a "sermon." The term *didaskein* is probably the broadest in meaning of all such verbs in that it describes "teaching," "instructing," or "imparting knowledge" by virtually any technique.

However, the concept of teaching in the early Christian community focused on the doctrine of Christ and church dogma, rather than the *kerygma* about Jesus which served as the core of the evangelistic message. According to Dodd, teaching consisted primarily of ethical instruction, exposition of scripture and theological doctrine, historical facts, and apologetics, most of which could be described as the apostolic tradition, or *paradosis*.[43] The contents of the New Testament, as well as other early Christian literature, reveal the practical nature of Christian teaching involving moral and ethical principles, and making application to every sphere of daily living.

In the apostolic church teaching was often accomplished by means of charismatic gifts, such as the gifts of prophecy and tongues. In such cases the information imparted must be regarded as inspired, rather than originating in the minds of teachers or being acquired from a study of authoritative sources. The exposition of scripture as a teaching technique was also employed in the early church, but was a carryover from Judaism and was maintained even after charismatic gifts disappeared.

From evidence previously discussed it can be deducted that the formal assembly of the early church included a period of teaching and preaching designed to edify the congregation. The structure of the assembly was based on that of the Jewish synagogue, and consequently included many of the Jewish concepts of propriety and order. Philo, who gives a description of a Jewish synagogue service, reveals that any capable individual could present a lesson or sermon. The term Philo used for "able" or "capable" was the standard term *empeirotatos*, meaning "the most experienced and appropriate."

This state of affairs sheds light on various New Testament passages concerning teaching. Hebrews 5:12 contains a reproach directed to those Christians who had enjoyed perhaps years of instruction, but were as yet incapable of teaching others. On the other hand, James 3:1 urges men to think carefully before becoming teachers, recognizing the hazards of such a responsible status. It does appear that in its earliest state the church knew a mutual teaching office in which the concepts of teaching and admonishing went hand in hand.

The Teacher

During the earliest days of the church teaching was the responsibility of the apostles, and the information they imparted can be attributed largely to Holy Spirit inspiration verified by miraculous "signs and wonders."[44] But with the endowment of charismatic gifts by laying on of apostolic hands, a class of inspired teachers appeared who played a vital role in the instruction of the Christian community. Teachers are first mentioned at Antioch, the first center of Gentile Christianity. Concerning the prophets and teachers of that church F.F. Bruce comments:

> As these prophets and teachers were carrying out their appointed ministry in the church, the Holy Spirit made known His will to them — doubtless through the prophetic utterance of one of their number.[45]

It is evident that as soon as the proportions of the growing church overcame the ability of the Twelve to supervise its teachings, additional Spirit-guided teachers were required. This ministry came to prevail in the church as a whole, at least till charismatic gifts died out sometime in the second century.

James deals extensively with the qualities of a wise teacher, as opposed to those who lack the humility and self-control to handle such a ministry, perhaps implying the same problem of self-exaltation as discussed by Paul in I Corinthians 12:14. In Galatians 5:5, probably the earliest of Paul's letters, mention is made of the need for amiable relationships between the congregation and its teachers. A number of scholars feel that this verse recommends the financial support of such teachers, implying that their work was regarded as a full-time ministry.[46] Therefore, the significant role played by teachers in the apostolic church is made evident by at least two very early New Testament works.

Another noteworthy text is I Corinthians 12:28, in which Paul lists teachers with apostles, prophets, and other charismatic, or Holy Spirit guided, ministries in the Corinthian church. There is general doubt as to whether the "pastors and teachers" of Ephesians 4:11 can be distinguished, but scholars feel certain that the Corinthians understood the work of apostles, prophets and evangelists to be that of instructing both the unconverted and converted, while pastors (elders, bishops) and teachers ministered almost solely to established congregations. In I Timothy 2:7 Paul refers to himself as a preacher, an apostle and a teacher, implying that his work covered every field of instruction.

Men could not serve as elders unless they were capable of teaching, and it may be that all church officers and leaders were required to exercise this ability. I Timothy 5:17 also states that elders who rule well should "be counted worthy of double honor, especially those who labor in the word and in teaching." The honor referred to here might be regarded as additional financial support, or "double pay," but the probable inference is that some elders did not engage in public ministry or in teaching.

Teachers, like prophets and tonguespeakers, were clearly not officers in the church, as were aspostles, elders and deacons, and the recognition given to teachers was one of function by means of acquired knowledge or by divine commission through charismatic gifts. It is for this reason that the Shepherd of Hermas distinguished four categories of church leaders:

> The stones that are squared and white, and that fit together in their joints, these are Apostles and bishops and teachers and deacons.[47]

The teaching concept in the early church might be outlined like this:

1. New Testament teaching was a mutually interchangeable function of the members of the congregation (Colossians 3:16; Romans 15:16).

2. It was done by means of a speech (homily), psalm, hymn, or spiritual song in the congregation (Ephesians 5:19; Colossians 3:16; I Corinthians 14).

3. This teaching contained the element of discussion and mutual admonition.

4. It could be done by a very large number of members (James 3:1).

5. It was permissible for many to do this as long as there was sufficient knowledge (Romans 15:14; Hebrews 5:12).

6. There was a rather large group of such people in every congregation (I Corinthians 12:28; Ephesians 4:11).

Women Teachers

The crucial passage concerning women teachers is I Timothy 2:12: "But I permit not a woman to teach nor to have dominion over a man, but to be in quietness."

The injunction of silence contained in this verse will be discussed later in a section related to the general deportment of Christian women. The question here is the apparent prohibition to teach. If Paul's statement in the first part of the verse is generalized, an alarming number of contradictions arise both in the history of the early church and in the practical application of New Testament principles. First, women are then forbidden to instruct their own children, which in fact was an integral part of education in most ancient cultures. Second, one would question Paul's commendation of Lois and Eunice for instructing Timothy from his childhood in holy scripture.[48] Third, one would be forced to reject Paul's advice to Titus to encourage older women to be:

> . . . teachers of that which is good; that they may train the younger women to love their husbands, to love their children, to be sober minded, chaste, workers at home, kind, being in subjection to their own husbands. . . .[49]

Fourth, one would be forced to question the commendation of Priscilla for her part in teaching Apollos a more perfect understanding of the will of God, in spite of his own eloquence and knowledge of the Hebrew scriptures.[50] It is clear that women in the early church did teach, were instructed to do so, and were commended for their efforts.

The difficulty, therefore, lies not in a prohibition to teach, but rather in the context of such teaching. As emphasized elsewhere, Paul's concern is for the behavior of women in light of social expediency as concerning subjection to men, or more specifically their own husbands. According to Ramsay any position of leadership or authority assigned to women in the church had to be avoided because of the tremendous pressure of custom:

> . . . in the existing state of Roman and Greek and Jewish society, people were not ready to accept women in the office of public teaching; nor had women in that society the education that was needed for such teaching.[51]

So strong was the feeling against women serving in the capacity of educators, that even the inspired prophetesses of Corinth had to be restrained from speaking in public assemblies. It is likely that on certain occasions secular knowledge could be imparted by a woman to a classroom of men, as did the Greeks, but such would not have been tolerated with regard to sacred scripture.

But there may be an even deeper thrust in this difficult prohibition. It cannot be ignored that the relationship between husbands and wives is a prominent subject in Pauline materials, and it may be that female prophetism interfered with traditional standards. The position of subordination assigned to wives in the Greco-Roman world, and reiterated by the early church leaders, would be violated if a wife found occasion to teach her husband, along with other men, in a public gathering.

The term *authentein* is an *hapax legomenon* in the New Testament, translated by the Authorized Version "to usurp authority over." Although Kittel has not included the term in his *Theological Dictionary*, several noted linguists have traced its etymology. The noun *authentes* is used by numerous classical writers to refer to an individual who commits suicide, or to a family murderer. Later, in Koine Greek, the idea of murder was dropped and the term came to describe an autocrat, lord, master, or potentate. The verb form then became a poignant and pithy expression meaning "to dictate to" or "play the boss over." In a marriage situation it would adequately describe a wife who by her own self-assertion dominates the husband.

Therefore, it would appear that Paul's prohibition was against women adopting a self-willed and domineering attitude, interfering in what was not properly their own domain, and thus trespassing established limits. The prevailing feeling was that woman's ideal lifestyle involved marrying, bearing children and being a keeper at home. Any action on the part of a woman which appeared to violate that position of willing subjection endangered the serenity of the *status quo*. In this light the passage should be understood "I do not allow a woman to teach, nor to be a dictator over, her husband."

Evidence suggests that in the early stages of the church certain women, along with a host of men, were endowed with charismatic gifts and thereby instructed outsiders in the Gospel and even prayed and prophesied in public assemblies. But problems arose due to certain violations of social propriety, resulting in friction between husbands and wives. In compliance with almost universal custom, wives were charged to conduct themselves in a manner of subjection and were prohibited to teach in any official capacity. They did, however, continue to teach privately, providing guidance and edification to men, women and children. Such a prohibition must be regarded as a concession to traditional male dominance, and does not preclude the possibility of female teachers given a conducive and mature environment.

5. Deportment of Women in the Apostolic Church

The books of the New Testament presuppose rather than express directly the fact that the Gospel arose in the midst of an ancient culture which continued to have a dramatic influence over the lives of early Christians. Believers were called by the Gospel message to separate themselves from the world in the sense of abandonment of former religious beliefs, striving to follow more elevated standards of conduct than perhaps before. But the New Testament contains hardly any precise information on the relations which they were to maintain toward the civilization, culture and secular institutions of their day.[1] Paul's letters to the Corinthians and Romans strongly suggest that social contact with non–Christian friends and acquaintances continued, although perhaps on a more cautious and ethics conscious plane. But details are lacking concerning the involvement of early Christians in government offices, military service, trade guilds, business partnerships, education, arts, athletics and entertainment.

There is a host of New Testament passages, some rather lengthy sections in the Epistles, which deal precisely with the ideal standard of conduct for Christians in face of skeptical, critical and often hostile surroundings. Jesus prepared his disciples to face persecution and hardship with the conviction that their exemplary lives as "the salt of the earth" and "the light of the world" would lead others to eternal life. His concept of sacrificial living, motivated by love, peace, compassion and purity, formed a significant part of the message which the apostles would take to the known world. The early community of believers was dominated by an ardent expectation of the Parousia with little time to waste on frivolities. Yet they were not so overwhelmed by this zeal as to lose sight of the mundane essentials of life and the necessity of expressing their convictions in the framework of cultural backgrounds. They still had families and friends who upheld other religious and social traditions; they still had to comply with state laws; and they still had to carry on business relations with pagans, rubbing shoulders with them in the streets and markets. And they themselves had to struggle against traditions and attitudes to which they had been slaves since childhood. Paul points out that it is in precisely this kind of environment that Christians can exert the greatest influence, not by austerity and seclusion, but by a positive effect upon the lives of individuals with whom they come in contact in daily routine activities.[2]

There is no question that New Testament exhortations to godly and exemplary living were directed at women as well as men. Considering the abundant evidence in historical sources that the conduct of women was of great social significance throughout the ancient world, and that women played prominent roles in the activities of the early Christian community, it is certain that the deportment of Christian women would have had bearing on the efficacy of the Gospel wherever the church was established.

Of the various subjects to be treated in this chapter, two are closely connected to the participation of women in church assembly: namely, Paul's injunction of silence, and wearing of veils. But all the subjects are related to one another in a fashion and can be approached most easily in a manner by which one leads naturally into another. The relationship between husbands and wives is a point of special concern throughout the New Testament, especially to Paul, and appears to be the underlying factor in the standards of conduct set for all Christian women. Therefore, this point will be discussed first.

I. MARRIAGE RELATIONSHIP

The institution of marriage is recognized by anthropologists as being an essential factor in the stability, and even the survival, of human societies. The family unit is a microcosm by which children are introduced to all the basic functions and mechanisms of their environment and assisted in adjusting to them. Sociologists regard the family as the basic unit of society and the initial means of transmitting human culture. In a treatment of social organization, Arensberg and Niehoff state:

> The whole idea is derived from the basic human institution of marriage, the uniting of two unrelated people to produce a third. So far is known, marriage and a family system has been almost universal, and two of the most basic functions seem to have been to bind together large numbers of people (the in-laws) and to rear children into the cultural system.[3]

The concept of marriage is introduced very early in the Bible and is portrayed as being of divine origin. The narrative describing Eve's formation from a rib of Adam served for the Jews as a beautiful and authoritative picture of God's intentions for the bond of love in monogamous marriage.

Jesus and Paul each emphasized the seriousness of the marriage bond by quoting Genesis 2:24 in opposition to the traditions contrived by the Jews to divorce for any cause. Clearly, from Old Testament principles and from the teaching of Jesus the early Christian community found solid grounds for rejecting social trends which tended to take marriage too lightly. Especially from the writings of Paul, the New Testament portrays the institution of marriage as a key to harmonious social relations within the Church community and an avenue of positive influence upon the pagan world. For this reason marriage and the home comprise the cornerstone of society and continue to receive the hallmark of approval in every culture.

Mutual Love

The concept of love is of great emphasis in the teaching of Jesus and the New Testament writers, and few would deny that one of the strongest bonds of love on a human level is that between a husband and wife. There is a significant difference between the terms for "love" used in the New Testament. The word *eros* expresses the lower type of animal passion, and *philos* a more elevated level of appreciation as brotherly love and affection. The highest form of love is expressed by the term *agape*, used to describe God's love for man (John 3:16) and the deepest level of love between people. The writer of Ephesians chooses this verb form to describe the love a Christian husband should have for his wife:

> Husbands, love your wives, just as Christ also loved the church and gave Himself up for her; husbands ought also to love their own wives as their own bodies. He who loves his own wife loves himself; for no one ever hated his own flesh, but nourishes and cherishes it, just as Christ also does the church . . .[4]

This analogy may have seemed extreme to Paul's original readers, but it has a significant purpose. As opposed to the cold formality of marriage simply to comply with family wishes or political expediency as was the norm in ancient cultures, marriage should be for love. Husbands should not view their wives as legal possessions, or fetish objects for gratifying lust, but should cherish them as Christ loved the body of believers for whom he died. Such love motivates a husband to labor to provide for the wife a suitable shelter, food and care. Defense and protection against intruders, or comfort in times of distress or sickness, is implied in Peter's words: "You husbands likewise, live with your wives in an understanding way, as with a weaker vessel since she is a woman . . ."[5]

Likewise wives are to love their husbands and make efforts to please them.[6] The advice of Paul in Titus 2:4 that young women must be "loving to their husbands, loving to their children and soberminded" was the voice of popular ethics in the first century depicting the ideal wife. The formula has been found on tombstone epitaphs and other memorial inscriptions at various ancient centers.[7] Although the ideal might have been sought after in the secular world, evidence has shown that true love between husbands and wives in the days of the early church was sadly lacking. Therefore, it is reasonable that a system such as Christianity, which sought the highest and noblest standards, would advocate the quality of love upon which good marriages are based.

Fidelity

The Greco-Roman world, including Jews of the Diaspora, suffered the results of lovelessness in marriages in the form of extreme infidelity, and many scholars think this problem to be among the symptoms of degeneration in any decaying society. In contrast, the early church encouraged faithfulness on the part of both partners in marriage and advocated principles which would lend stability to society as a whole. Paul's discussion of fornication in his first letter to Corinth includes a mandate that fornication was out of character for any child of God, and that every man and woman should have a marital partner in order to avoid illicit sexual relationships. Paul's personal preference seems to have been to remain single, no doubt because his motivations were almost totally centered in evangelism. But he recognized that the average individual might not have his ability to curb the sexual appetite, and advised the unmarried and widows to marry if they could not control the natural desire.[8] He never wrote disparagingly about marriage. In fact the beauty and holiness of marriage is one of the apostle's frequent subjects, and sexual fidelity to one's partner is almost a presupposition. There is a distinction in the New Testament between the terms "adultery" and "fornication." The former relates specifically to marital infidelity, the violation of marital vows through intercourse with another party. The latter appears to relate to any illicit sexual relationship, including homosexuality, and is derived from the concept of prostitution. It also appears that sex in marriage is the only acceptable gratification of sexual desire in the New Testament,[9] with the exception of masturbation, which is never mentioned in either Old or New Testaments.[10]

Conjugal Rights

The implication is clear that the solidity of a marriage depends to a large extent on the sexual relationship of the two partners. In fact, other than providing the ideal environment for child-rearing, the primary motivation for marriage is sex. Therefore, rendering conjugal rights becomes a duty to which a Christian marriage partner is bound. Paul instructs:

> Let the husband fulfill his duty to his wife, and likewise also the wife to her husband. The wife does not have authority over her own body, but the husband does; and likewise also the husband does not have authority over his own body, but the wife does. Stop depriving one another, except by agreement for a time that you may devote yourselves to prayer, and come together again lest Satan tempt you because of your lack of self-control.[11]

Ideally the experience should be an uninhibited and open expression of love for the full gratification of both partners. Modern psychology has discovered sexual frustration to be at the root of many emotional disorders, and such was probably the case in ancient cultures as well.

Separation and Divorce

Consideration has been given already to the question of divorce as treated by both Jesus and Paul. But something must be said about the practical application of these directives by early Christians. Two areas of stress are evident.

There can be little doubt that critical times, especially for Christians under persecution, and the changes in political and social environs intensified the problem of marital incompatibility to the degree that many Christian couples viewed divorce as the only solution to their difficulties. For these Paul made allowance for temporary separation, if circumstances became unbearable, with a view to reconciliation when differences were resolved.

But a problem more difficult to address was that of unhappy marriages between Christians and unbelievers. Because the principles of their faith opposed divorce, regardless of circumstances, Christians married to either Jewish or pagan partners were almost at their mercy if marital problems developed, divorce being common in the Greco-Roman world. It seems that certain believers had falsely concluded, no doubt in self-defense, that if a Christian was unable to convert his or her partner a legal divorce could be sought under the assumption that the marriage was non-existent in the sight of God. But Paul contends that such marriages are valid. His argument that otherwise the children would be illegitimate proves nothing, but has a strong emotional appeal. Besides maintaining such a marriage for the sake of the children he argues that by remaining faithful to the marriage the believer might win the unbelieving partner to Christianity.[12] Peter echoes these sentiments specifically with regard to the conduct of Christian wives:

... If any of them are disobedient to the word, they may be won without a word by the behavior of their wives, as they observe your chaste and respectful behavior.[13]

It is also possible that very early certain groups had incorporated the Mosaic concession into the teachings of Christ and then came to regard desertion by a pagan partner as tantamount to adultery, thereby establishing legitimate grounds for divorce and remarriage.

It would be foolish to argue that a discontent Jew, Greek or Roman married to a Christian would not seek legal divorce, for evidence already examined suggests otherwise. But the apostle, now representing a higher standard and a more noble view of marriage, seeks to preserve marriages rather than seeking grounds for dissolving them. The expression "not under bondage" cannot be taken to mean "not under a law binding him to the marriage," as understood by some. Rather, Paul is stating that the Christian has done all he or she can do to preserve the marriage and cannot, under such circumstances, be bound to the whims of the pagan partner. Christians, rather than leaving their faith in bondage to marriage, might have to resign themselves to divorce and let their partners do as they choose. Though some see in this an implied right of remarriage, Paul in reality does not address that issue. The absence of examples of the church dealing directly with complex marital entanglement leaves the impression that early Christians left judgment on such matters to God alone.

Marriage to a Non-Believer

Most of what Paul says with regard to marriage in I Corinthians 7 involves Christians with non–Christian husbands or wives. It is apparent, however, that he approaches such marital incompatibility as if the couples involved were married before the one partner was converted to Christianity, in which case Paul advises if at all possible to live together in harmony: "Let each man remain in that condition in which he was called."[14] Another question arises from a statement in Paul's second letter to Corinth, perhaps having been made orally to the same group at an earlier stage: "Do not be bound together with unbelievers; for what partnership have righteousness and lawlessness, or what fellowship has light with darkness?"[15] The apostle does not relate his advice only to marriage, but to every sphere of intimate association with worldly and evil people. Nevertheless, the strongest bond to which Paul could allude is that of marriage, and the metaphor in *heterogzugountes* doubtless comes from Deuteronomy 22:10, where among other unnatural combinations, plowing with an ox and an ass harnessed together is prohibited.[16] In ancient usage the term seems to relate especially to mixed marriages, and the Septuagint translation of Leviticus

19:19 indicates that the root meaning of the term pertains to mating or inter-breeding livestock. Therefore, there can be little doubt that in this statement the apostle was discouraging Christians from entering into marriage with non-believers — for such marriages would be neither immoral or invalid, but simply difficult, strained by conflicting norms and values.

Right of Marriage in General

The New Testament makes no prohibitions of marriage, except those implied in cases of divorce for no legitimate cause, and here implications are questioned by many exegetes. Paul encourages the unmarried who feel the desire for a sexual companion to marry. The right of remarriage is extended to widows and is implied in cases of divorced persons, if the divorce was on grounds of adultery.[17] Paul defends the right of apostles to marry if they so choose, and seems to include marriage among the qualifications for the offices of bishop and deacon.[18] Celibacy, either voluntary or mandatory for religious reasons, is unknown in the Bible except for allusions by Jesus in Matthew 19:12 and Paul in I Corinthians 7:8. In fact, Paul's fearful vision of an imminent falling away identified one facet of that heresy as the prohibition of marriage, although he did not indicate to whom such a prohibition might apply.[19] There are no examples in the New Testament of anyone being forbidden to marry, whether a Christian having become involved in immorality, a divorced person seeking salvation or a sincere Christian wishing to devote himself completely to the Lord's service. Any such prohibition arises not from scripture but from the human tendency to codify and regulate.

Female Subjection in Marriage

While the ontological inferiority of women has remained almost universally accepted until the present century, even among mainstream Christian denominations, the New Testament does not actually support this notion. In fact, one would be hard pressed to find anything in the New Testament to suggest that women as a class are to be subject to men as a class. Rather, in most if not every case where the subject arises the writer is in reality speaking of the relationship of husbands and wives. As one examines Pauline passages, for instance, it becomes progressively clearer that female subjection has meaning only in the context of marital roles, and Paul's suggestions pertain strictly to his conception of the ideal Christian housewife behaving herself quietly and unobtrusively, yielding gracefully to her husband as head of the family. In Paul's day the married woman was classified as "one subject to a man," apart from whatever social inferiority she was thought to have by virtue of being a woman. But Paul's frequent expression *aner kai gunaikos*, generally translated "man and woman," quite clearly has the limited connotation of "husband and wife." But this cannot be said of Greek literature in general. It simply seems to be a unique application among various New Testament writers. And the reason is simply a subtle compliance with social expediency, but with enough refinement so as to display and create a propensity for spiritual growth on a social level.

Therefore, the role which the Christian wife should play, according to Paul, Peter, and others, has special religious and social significance.

I Corinthians 11:3, 8

Of paramount importance is the use of the term "head" in Paul's treatment of the hierarchy of God, Christ, man and woman. The term *kephale* basically refers to the physical appendage called the head, and is so used in verse 4. But throughout the section of verses 3–10, and elsewhere in the New Testament, the word has a double meaning.

Many ancients recognized the head to be the center of thought, motivation and physical coordination, and therefore the governing faculty of the body. Paul in this passage utilizes a concept familiar to him from both Hebrew and Greek, that when one imposes his will upon another, or holds a position of authority over another, the second party can be thought of as subordinate to the first as "his head." Therefore, to illustrate the subordinate role of a wife to her husband, Paul says: "Christ is the head of every man, and the man is the head of a woman, and God is the head of Christ."

The passage should not be understood to stratify the four beings in order of power or importance. If this had been the writer's intention a more appropriate approach would be to list them beginning with God and ending with the woman. Nor does the passage pertain to men and women as classes, but rather to the relationship between a husband and wife.

Paul does suggest an analogy between Christ's origin with God, apart from the New Testament assertion of Christ's eternal nature, and woman's origin with man. The basis for subordination of the wife, he says, lies in the creation. According to one rendition of the origin of humanity in Genesis the male was brought into being first. But the absence of a suitable mate among the animals necessitated the creation of a human female, Eve, formed from the rib of Adam.[20] The name "Adam" signifies the ground from which man was formed, and "Eve" symbolizes that woman would be the mother of all living humans to come. The Hebrew word for man, *ish*, actually expresses the idea of mankind, including the female. And the term *ishah* is merely the feminine of *ish*, and does not necessarily imply that woman was taken out of man as suggested in Genesis 2:23. But this explanation of the origin of woman is clearly the basis for Hebrew thinking on the subordination of wives, and is so used by the Apostle Paul.

The rabbis explained Eve's origin in the following fashion:

> God said: I will not create her from the head that she should not hold
> up her head too proudly: nor from the eye that she should not be a co-
> quette: nor from the ear that she should not be an eavesdropper: nor
> from the mouth that she should not be too talkative: nor from the heart
> that she should not be too jealous: nor from the hand that she should not
> be too acquisitive: nor from the foot that she should not be a gadabout:
> but from a part of the body which is hidden that she should be modest.

But they added that it was all to no effect, since women are basically
greedy, lazy, jealous, garrulous and are compulsive eavesdroppers.[21] So it
seems that while they felt compelled to take the rib story literally the rabbis
could not help suspecting that somehow, somewhere in the process God
made some kind of error, either in production or in design.

As far as can be determined, the view that male and female were
created simultaneously as partners, opposites designed to complement each
other, never found credence among the Hebrews in spite of the implications
of the first chapter of Genesis. But modern scholarship is forced to view
critically a literal interpretation of the Adam and Eve story in order to
distinguish between divine principle and Hebrew legend, and it is very
likely that the difference between the first and second creation account in
Genesis is highly significant to the study of female subjection.

I Timothy 2:11b, 13-14

> Let the woman learn in quietness with all subjection. For Adam was
> first formed, then Eve. And Adam was not deceived, but the woman be-
> ing deceived was in transgression.

The significant term translated "subjection" appears several times in
Paul's writings concerning the status of women, and is used by Peter as
well.[22] According to lexicographers the term is used in classical Greek
militarily, meaning to "rank," "to place under" or "to subordinate." It is
clearly the married woman to whom Paul directs these remarks, as in I Corinthians 11, and the issue is propriety in view of her subordinate role in
marriage. Some kind of tension seems to have arisen which necessitated an
authoritative reminder concerning the respect and reverence which a married woman owes her husband. Of course, while these texts might relate
specifically to problems having arisen in church assemblies, there is little
doubt that the principle was understood by the recipients of Paul's letter to
apply to every sphere of their lives.

It is not fair to push Paul's arguments to the extreme in relation to the
Fall. The deception of Eve does not imply intellectual inferiority on her

part, nor can such be used as evidence for the ontological inferiority of women. The apostle simply employs this historical illustration to suggest that wives should allow their husbands to play the role of leadership, both in the social aspects of marriage and in the spiritual guidance of the home. Paul refrains from mentioning that Adam accepted Eve's offer of the "forbidden fruit" without question and in total disregard of the instructions of God. The problem in the Genesis account of the Fall was not so much the deception of Eve as the failure on the part of Adam to exercise his authority over her in light of her apparent imperception. Wives cannot justly be blamed for failure to subject themselves to authority which their husbands do not exercise. But it is not the husband's side of the issue which Paul emphasizes, perhaps implying that the predominant difficulty among early Christian husbands and wives existed in the unwillingness of some women to accept the subordinate role in marriage. It might also suggest the difficulty husbands were having in coping with the changes Christianity brought about in relationships and the liberty afforded their wives in Christ. In either case Paul's advice leans toward tradition.

A similar injunction occurs in Titus 2:5, where Paul encourages the older women to teach younger wives their responsibilities, which included "being subject to their own husbands." The impact of Christian example in every community must have been far-reaching and of utmost importance in converting pagans to Christ, for Paul adds that women should play this role properly so that "the word of God may not be dishonored."

Ephesians 5:22–24

> Wives, be subject to your own husbands, as to the Lord. For the husband is the head of the wife, as Christ also is head of the Church, he himself being the Savior of the body. But as the church is subject to Christ, so also the wives ought to be to their husbands in everything.

Most English versions incorrectly translate verse 22, inserting "be subject," which does not occur at this place in the best manuscripts. Therefore, it is clear that the force of Paul's admonition to wives comes from the use of a participle in the previous verse, where the apostle makes a general statement, "In thanks and reverence to God be subject to each other." But a close parallel to this verse is found in Colossians 3:17–18, in which Paul writes:

> And whatever you do in word or deed, do all in the name of the Lord Jesus, giving thanks through Him to God the Father. Wives, be subject to your husbands, as is fitting in the Lord.

Here the term "be subject" is employed with direct reference to the wives as fitting or expected by social norms. The addition of "in the Lord" is very

much like Paul's advice to masters and slaves, that social obligations must
be met, not because of respect people might be due or deserve, but because
it is right in the sight of God. But the injunction is followed by an admonition to husbands to love their wives, very much the same as expressed in
Ephesians 5, but including the advice "be not bitter against them." It is unfortunate that the English terms "subject" and "subjection" are generally
employed here in that they convey the idea of slavery or tyranny. The intention, rather, is to express the man's headship over the family with the
marriage understood as a corporate unity. But even so, Paul could not help
having the patriarchal family order as a backdrop to his thinking, and this
was in conformity with the customs of most of the world in the first Christian century including codes of domestic behavior.

I Peter 3:1

> In the same way, you wives, be submissive to your own husbands so
> that even if any of them are disobedient to the word, they may be won
> without a word by the behavior of their wives.

This advice, traditionally ascribed to Peter, closely parallels Pauline doctrine. The adverb "in the same way" must be taken closely with the injunction "be submissive" from the previous chapter, implying that just as slaves
are to show honor to and subject themselves to their masters so Christian
wives are to respect traditional subjection to their husbands.

A question might be raised as to why the New Testament, and
especially Paul, speaks so persistently of the married state and makes little
or no allowance for the single male and female, particularly considering
that the apostle himself was single. The complex cultural backgrounds to
the New Testament provide an explanation.

First, single women of a marriageable age were almost non-existent.
Girls married at an early age in Roman, Greek and Jewish cultures, and if
widowed while still young would generally be approached by some suitor
for remarriage. Second, celibacy and perpetual virginity were rare, and
were not held in high esteem except in unusual groups such as the Essenes,
or among special classes of religious devotees such as the Roman Vestal
Virgins. Third, in the Greco-Roman world women were generally regarded
as under the legal authority or guardianship of some man, whether father,
elder brother, uncle or husband. For any New Testament writer to deal extensively with rare exceptions and hypothetical cases would be contrary to
its appeal to the masses and its sympathy with the standards of propriety
in various cultures. Therefore, concerning the status of married women the
New Testament strongly upholds the principle of subordination to the
husband, and dwells on that theme because of its universal appeal. In
fact it is noteworthy that major sections of Pauline writings deal with

the more common relationships of most societies: husband and wife, parent and child and master and slave, the last of which translates into today's context as employer and employee. In all of them he teaches the principle of love and mutual respect.

Concerning those passages which deal specifically with husbands and wives, the crucial point is whether the hierarchy of husband as head of the wife is actually ordained of God and a divinely authoritative universal rule. The traditional approach to this issue is to see the dominant role of the husband as a natural axiom to biological distinctions between the human male and female. This approach holds that God structured the marriage to comply with the natural order of things, and to fit the general pattern of every human society.

This view has come under fire in recent years as women have achieved social equality and have proved themselves the equals of men in many fields of endeavor. The basis for an alternate view on these crucial passages will be presented in the final chapter. But it is critical to note that the traditional interpretation is determined almost totally by approaching scripture with certain preconceptions about inspiration, and with a predilection for fundamental adherence to scripture. This hermeneutic is proving to be a major stumblingblock in resolving the modern dilemma concerning the status of women in the church.

II. SAVED IN CHILDBEARING

A passage which should be mentioned on its own is I Timothy 2:15, in which Paul states: "But women shall be preserved through the bearing of children if they continue in faith and love and sanctity with self-restraint." In the two verses which precede this statement to Timothy, the apostle points to the creation narrative, emphasizing the order in which man and woman were formed and the fact of Eve's deception in order to strengthen his argument for female subordination in marriage. He then turns to a positive aspect of female subjection and abandons the illustration of Eve for a final statement concerning Christian women in general. There are two principal interpretations of this verse.

The first is that in spite of woman's foolish deception which brought sin into the world, specifically through Eve, woman became the essential instrument for producing the Savior, specifically the childbearing of Mary. This view was suggested by an anonymous medieval commentator, revived by Ellicott, von Soden and Wohlenberg, and upheld by a few modern scholars.[23]

The second view is that childbearing, including the rearing and instruction of children and keeping of the home, is the highest ideal in

Christian womanhood and is the lifestyle by which a Christian wife attains eternal life. The fact that Paul frequently discusses womanhood in terms of marital responsibilities, and the fact that in the immediate context he deals with the subordinate demeanor of wives as opposed to the behavior of wives who dominate and "play the boss over" their husbands, would favor this interpretation. This in no way suggests that salvation is dependent upon fertility, nor that marriage and childbearing are a requirement for every woman. But rather, the apostle employs an expression which embraces the entire role of a woman who submits to the duties of marriage.

By playing that role well, she has a far greater potential for influencing mankind toward Christianity, and for obtaining her own salvation, than by attempting to dominate her husband and playing the role of a teacher. In short, these words represent Paul's attempt to lend dignity and spiritual worth to motherhood. Paul also emphasizes in his first letter to Corinth that the married Christian woman should be devoted to pleasing her husband, a duty overshadowed only by her allegiance to the will of God where the two might be in conflict.[24]

III. THE INJUNCTION OF SILENCE

Of critical significance with regard to the conduct of women in the church assembly is the apparent injunction of silence in I Corinthians 14:34–35 and I Timothy 2:11–12. Having concluded that women did participate in certain forms of leadership in the assembly, at least through the exercise of spiritual gifts, it becomes necessary to reconcile that fact with the above-mentioned passages. But the subject will be discussed at this point because it relates to, and is dependent upon, the overwhelming significance of the marriage relationship among Christians and to the significance of female deportment as a tool for upholding and propagating the Gospel.

Scholarship is clearly divided concerning the passages in question, some holding to the silence injunction and attempting to explain away the possibility of women praying and prophesying publicly, while others defend the latter and try to explain away the silence injunction.

Perhaps a solution can be found which lends credence to both statements without suggesting change of mind on the part of Paul, and which avoids simply ignoring or disregarding whichever of the passages appears the most problematic.

I Corinthians 14:33-35

> For God is not a God of confusion but of peace, as in all the churches of the saints. Let the women keep silent in the churches; for they are not permitted to speak, but let them subject themselves, just as the Law also says. And if they desire to learn anything, let them ask their own husbands at home; for it is improper for a woman to speak in church.

Recent scholarship has tended to remove this segment of the text, primarily on the basis of its apparent conflict with I Corinthians 11, arguing that this section was somehow interpolated into an early manuscript from some other source. The only textual issue concerning the passage is that a small group of insignificant manuscripts, mostly western, transpose verses 34-35 to follow verse 40, apparently to place them under the heading of *order in the church* rather than *prophecy*. There is no solid evidence that the verses are a later addition or gloss. Manuscript testimony suggests the existence of the verses in accepted texts before the appearance of texts omitting them. Therefore, one must conclude that the present form of the text is as close to Paul's own wording as we are capable of establishing, and both sections appeared in the original letter we call I Corinthians. This being the case, there must be a suitable explanation for Paul's command of silence which compliments, rather than contradicts, I Corinthians 11.

There is evidence that the verb *lalein* refers to conversational talk, jabbering or chattering as might be done at a party or social gathering.[25] Apparently, Chrysostom was confronted with a situation in church services of his own time, the late fourth century, in which women were given to much talking and conversing with one another. But in I Corinthians 14 the term appears eighteen times, in each case with the sense of "speaking with a view to communicating a message," and in most cases it clearly relates to public address. Besides, in verse 28 there appears a command of silence on the part of those who were addressing the congregation in a charismatic tongue when no interpreter was present and no one could understand the language. Under such circumstances the speaker should "keep silence in the church, and let him speak to himself and to God."

The answer seems to lie in verse 35. As is frequently the case, Paul's concern is for standards of propriety with regard to the socially accepted subordination of wives to their husbands, as whatever might tend to disrupt that pattern would create unnecessary friction both in the home and in the local social structure. Verse 35 indicates that the problem involved questions which the women were asking during the assembly. Verses 26-35 are clearly a single paragraph and deal with the problem of prophets and tonguespeakers speaking out of turn, simultaneously or when the content had no constructive value. As in other places Paul uses the terms *aner kai gunaikos* with general reference to husband and wife relationships, here more specifically in the context of their roles as prophets, prophetesses and tonguespeakers. Therefore the injunction of silence pertains to an abuse of spiritual gifts by prophetesses in overstepping the bounds of propriety to the degree of offensiveness in the assembly. Abuse of spiritual gifts and misunderstanding of even basic practices such as the Lord's Supper was a major cause for writing this letter. And it appears that those women who had been functioning as prophetesses began to disrupt the assembly and embarrass their husbands by repeatedly firing questions at whichever speaker had the floor, perhaps even assisting those whose role it was to judge the validity of each prophecy. In so doing they assumed the anomalous role of judging men, and refused to cooperate with their husbands' insistence that they should be quiet. In opposition to such conduct Paul suggests that they be quiet, and ask questions at home rather than disturbing the assembly with contentious and silly questions.

Since the circumstances here are unique, clearly related to spiritual gifts not functioning today, this hardly becomes a precedent for a universal law prohibiting women from speaking in church assembly. Even among Charismatics where certain spiritual gifts are imitated today the key issue is propriety in conduct, not whether a woman is actually speaking publicly. Besides, the fact that Paul appeals to the Law of Moses in a letter addressed to a predominantly Gentile church betrays a lingering Jewish mentality which was destined to give way to a broader spirit emulating the mind of Jesus Christ.

I Timothy 2:11–12

> Let a woman quietly receive instruction with entire submissiveness.
> But I do not allow a woman to teach or exercise authority over a man,
> but to remain quiet.

The key term here is *hesuchia*. It should be noted that the translation "silence" which appears in the Authorized Version in both verses 11 and 12 has led to mistaken application of this passage. As opposed to the command to "be quiet" in I Corinthians 14:34, Paul here is speaking about the general character of a godly woman, leading a quiet and peaceful life rather than clamoring for attention in boisterous rebellion of all acceptable standards of conduct. A.T. Robertson suggests that the simplest and most common meaning is "in all subjection."[26] The intent of the apostle, therefore, was not to enjoin upon women a law of silence in religious assemblies but to uphold the ideal of the Christian housewife in all activities. Besides, it is not clear whether these comments pertain to a public church assembly or to private circumstances and interpersonal conflict.

But there is reason to think that Paul is speaking specifically with regard to husbands and wives. He forcefully expresses the violation of expected subjection of wives, namely through the unusual term *authentein*, which appears to be a pithy colloquialism very nearly equivalent to the modern expression "wearing the pants."[27] The clear violation of propriety, of which the wives in question were guilty, was in "playing the boss" over their husbands. To be in quietness means to remain within the established limits of social expediency.

IV. ADORNING

According to Laver, anthropologists have exploded the idea held by westerners that clothing originated in an impulse of modesty, as well as the alternative theory of dress for protection from the elements. Instead, it is now believed that male clothing, in primitive, ancient and modern societies alike, is based on a hierarchial principle, while female garb has followed a principle of seduction.[28] This means simply that the underlying psychological motive for male dress is to provide a sense of superiority or dominance over other males. A feather in one's cap both increases apparent height and augments self-confidence; a headdress, necklace or armband symbolizes status, dexterity at craft, victory in battle or prowess in hunting. Female clothing, on the other hand, is based on the principle of decorating and hiding certain parts of the body in order to call attention to them, and thus to eroticize that portion of the body and increase its attractiveness to the opposite sex. It is not, therefore, the taking off of clothes which has had erotic significance so much as the covering up and decorating what John Flugel has called "the shifting erogenous zones." This being the case, one can appreciate the significance of female dress in the early Christian community. From the teaching of Jesus, and before that the Old Testament, it is obvious that in Judaism the female body was naturally alluring to the male, and anyone desiring to maintain a godly pattern of life must guard against the arousal of sexual passion toward a female who is not his legitimate sex partner. While Christian men have to guard their own minds against inordinant desires which might lead to fornication or adultery, women are responsible for dressing in such a manner as to avoid inducing or inviting a lustful gaze.

In addition to the erotic principle there is also the problem of overdressing from the standpoint of vanity and egocentricity. The lavish adornment of Roman women had developed beyond eroticism and was motivated largely from the desire to outdo other women.

As to what might be termed immodest in these ancient cultures, New Testament passages speak in detail. The writers Paul and Peter give advice which reflects the problem of gaudy dress typical of women of fashion in the first century and also which verifies the theory of Flugel.

I Timothy 2:9–10

> Likewise, I want women to adorn themselves with proper clothing, modestly and discreetly, not with braided hair and gold or pearls or costly garments; but rather by means of good works, as befits women making a claim to godliness.

Some commentators hold that Paul's concern was not so much dress which displayed Christian character in daily living, but rather that attire which was suitable for worship services. While the context contains references to praying, teaching and the silence of women, all of which might relate to common traditions concerning formal worship, the thrust of New Testament doctrine pertains to the influence of Christians in their daily routine, with little if any focus on special occasions. Cyprian, bishop of Carthage writing around A.D. 250, said in exposition of this passage:

> The characteristics of ornaments, and of garments, and the allurements of beauty, are not fitting for any but prostitutes and immodest women. . . . Let chaste and modest virgins avoid the dress of the unchaste, the manners of the immodest, the ensigns of brothels, the ornaments of harlots.[29]

John Chrysostom, representing Syrian theology of the late fourth century, said that such attire as Paul warned against was the gaudy dress of "actors and dancers that live upon the stage." An additional statement by Chrysostom relates his thinking to that of Cyprian: "Imitate not therefore the courtesans; for by such a dress they allure their many lovers and hence many have incurred a disgraceful suspicion."[30]

There is no New Testament doctrine concerning special garb for Christians in worship, for it seems that both Jesus and his apostles understood that whatever is proper for daily routine is proper for the assembly of believers. In fact, the whole tenor of Jesus' instruction on prayer and special devotions is that God is concerned with human heart, and not with outward appearance.

The modern western mind thinks of immodest dress as that which exposes too much of the body. While this certainly would be included in those considerations of modesty by Christians, such does not seem to be the primary problem in Paul's day. In fact, no New Testament writer makes any direct reference to scanty clothing or nudity. The earliest known references to such occur in the *Apostolic Constitutions* and deal with women bathing with men at the local bath houses.[31]

In Paul's day the major concern seems to be gaudy, extravagant and costly dress, as well as excessive make-up and lavish jewelry. And it would appear that standards of modesty are understood by New Testament writers, and should be so understood by us, to be determined to a large degree by social norms, rather than by an innate human conscience or by divinely revealed standards.

The terminology in I Timothy 2:9 is poorly represented by the Authorized Version, but when translated correctly displays the flexibility of standards of modesty from a Christian perspective. The adjective *kosmios*, often rendered "modest," is better translated "orderly." The noun *aidos*, translated "shamefacedness" in the Authorized Version, means "modesty" in the sense of reverence, awe and respect for the feelings and opinions of others, for one's own conscience and for the customs of his or her society. The term translated "sobriety" is *sophrosune*, meaning "sensible, with discretion and soundness of mind."

While all these terms may be somewhat imprecise when isolated from a specific context, the apostle explains himself with the phrase: "not with braided hair, or gold or pearls or costly garments."

The real point is that the Christian woman should not be motivated by a desire to call attention to herself, or to outdo other women in dress or in physical beauty. Her concern should not be for external beauty at all, but for the qualities of character which are the fruit of the spirit of Christ.

I Peter 3:3–5

> And let not your adornment be merely external; braiding the hair and wearing gold jewelry, or putting on dresses; but let it be the hidden person of the heart, with the imperishable quality of a gentle and quiet spirit, which is precious in the sight of God. For in this way in former times the holy women also, who hoped in God, used to adorn themselves, being submissive to their own husbands.

No term is used by Peter in this passage which could be translated "modest," but the overall tone is the same as the Pauline text discussed above. There is, of couse, no intrinsic wrong in braiding the hair, wearing jewelry or dressing in expensive garments. And it is not the purpose of Peter or Paul to so imply. But the emphasis of life for a godly woman should be mode of living and inner character, as opposed to the vanity and shallowness of artificial feminine pulchritude.

V. HEADCOVERINGS

The possible requirement of headcoverings, or veils, to be worn by Christian women hinges on one New Testament passage, I Corinthians 11:2–16, the interpretation of which is the subject of considerable scholastic debate.

There are, in fact, several interpretive difficulties with this passage. The concept of women "praying and prophesying" has already been discussed in another chapter. At this point, the primary question is whether Paul required the veiling of women in the assembly and perhaps in public, and on what grounds such an injunction could have been issued. If not, then some alternative interpretation of the passage must be sought.

The Doctrine of Tertullian

It is commonly accepted that various church traditions enjoining upon women the wearing of a veil or some other artificial headcovering in worship have their roots in this single Pauline text. But the earliest exegete known to interpret it in this fashion is Tertullian. The writings of this church father represent the orthodox tradition in North Africa around the end of the second century, and include a lengthy exegesis of the passage in question with special concern for the wearing of veils.[32] Tertullian accepted that I Corinthians 11 deals only with married women, and that even this passage is doubtful as a proof text for the strict doctrine which he advocated. Nevertheless, he strongly believed that all women, especially virgins of a marriageable age, should veil themselves to avoid the lustful gaze of men. He defined the area to be covered by the veil as "the space covered by the hair when unbound; in order that the necks may be encircled," but elsewhere in the same work he implied that the face should be covered as well. It is clear that to Tertullian a virtuous Christian wife could be identified by her covered head, just as a virgin could symbolize her purity by wearing a veil.

However, it is equally clear that the practice of headcovering as Tertullian defined it was only arising as a church tradition in his own time. He alludes to the former customs, doubtless in the previous generation, in which the matter of veiling was left entirely to the individual, just as it was her choice to marry, and he recognizes that customs varied extensively from one place to another. Of the Arabian women Tertullian writes that they covered both head and face, with one eye free, so as to see rather than to be seen. In addition, he quotes an unnamed Roman woman of nobility as stating that veiled women, who dressed differently from her own custom, could "More easily fall in love than be fallen in love with." In one place he says "at this day the Corinthians do veil their virgins; what the apostles taught their disciples approve." Tertullian claims that in his day the majority of churches kept their virgins veiled, but he admits that in the first century the Corinthians were exceptions because they wore veils. Even this he may have misunderstood, and evidence is lacking from the first century to support his claim.

While it is certain that Tertullian expected Christian women to observe his ideals, such was not the case in his own community, which indicates that veiling as he defined it was neither a natural inclination nor a social norm in his day. Concerning the Christian assembly he speaks of those women who deserve chastisement because they are "uncovered" during the recital of psalms and at the mention of the name of God. He continues by ridiculing those who have a fringe, a tuft, the palm of the hand, or any thread whatever to place upon the crown of their heads at such times and thereby consider themselves covered.

In spite of the apparent unpopularity of the doctrine, and its peculiarity to certain localities, the tradition so strongly urged by Tertullian became almost universally accepted in the church during the centuries which followed.[33]

Paul's Terminology

Upon one's first encounter with this passage, the application made of it by Tertullian and later church fathers might appear to be the only logical one. But the terminology chosen by Paul suggests that something other than an artificial veil or headcovering was the point of discussion; namely hair.

The most common Greek term for veil, *kalumma*, is rare in the New Testament, and its absence from this passage is conspicuous. Most of the terms which Paul employs have the same root as *kalumma*, but the fact that he avoids the specific noun, making use instead of a variety of more complex constructions, would indicate that something other than the traditional veil was the subject and that his audience understood him perfectly.

The first expression, *kata kephales echon* (v.4), translated literally means "having something down from the head." It appears only once in this passage, is used with reference to the headcovering of men, and is thought by some to refer to the Jewish "tallith." The majority of Paul's expressions taken as suggestive of a veil are derived from *katakaluptein*, the intensive form of *kaluptein*, meaning "to hide," "to conceal," "to bury" or "to cover."[34] In classical Greek the same term is employed with reference to a variety of coverings, and is only associated with the head or face if so stated. Such also is the case in the Septuagint. The only noun used by the apostle with reference to the "covering" of a woman's head is *peribolaion*, and this Paul suggests is the function of her hair. The word suggests that which is thrown around, and its appearances in classical literature and the Septuagint are numerous. According to lexicographers, it can describe anything from a bed cover to a covering for the legs and feet, dressing gown, shawl, warm enveloping garment for outdoors, or hood of any sort for covering the head on public occasions. Basically, the noun and verb forms refer to "throwing around a garment."

The majority of modern scholars take the above-mentioned group of terms as descriptive of a cloth veil which Paul requires for Christian women when in worship or devotion.[35] This approach generally regards Paul's appeal to the shameful violation of nature, his suggestion that an "unveiled woman" may as well be shaven and shorn and finally his appeal to woman's hair as a covering, as illustrative and supportive arguments employed by the apostle to validate his injunction. There is the possibility, however, that the mention of woman's hair was the climax of the discussion and in fact the root of the problem. But before this alternative is investigated, numerous flaws and inconsistencies in the traditional view should be noted.

Headcoverings in Ancient Cultures

In order for Paul's instructions to relate to artificial headcoverings, one is forced to apply the prohibition as strongly to men as to women. Whatever is required of women must be forbidden to men in order to carry out the instructions sensibly and consistently. And, if the arguments concerning nature, or custom, and hair are valid, one must look for verification in the veiling and headcovering customs of the cultures most closely related to the circumstances in which the apostle wrote. On both these points, however, evidence leads to the conclusion that in neither Jewish, Roman nor Greek customs was there a stigma attached to men having covered heads, nor was it required that women cover their heads, in worship.

The earliest record of the use of some kind of veil in the Old Testament is the shawl of Rebekah. This passage states that Rebekah "covered herself ... then Isaac brought her into the tent...; and she became his wife."[36]

According to the Assyrian code, dated by Miles and Driver around 1500 B.C., veiling was an essential part in legalizing a marriage among many bedouins of the Near East, symbolizing property rights over the wife.[37] The Code also prohibits a harlot to be seen wearing a veil, which is quite contrary to the impression left by the record of Judah's encounter with Tamar in which he took her to be a harlot because her face was covered.[38]

Because of the scarcity of relevant passages in the Old Testament it is impossible to form any definitive conclusions about the significance of veiling during this long period. A few references to "covering the head" are made in apocryphal literature, attributed to the intertestamental period, but the terminology is as indistinct as that of I Corinthians 11, and like the Old Testament references, little can be concluded from them.

Roland de Vaux is probably correct in stating that Jewish women did not wear a veil over the face, as associated with the oriental custom, although they may on occasions have had their heads or faces partly covered in other ways.[39] But there is far greater evidence to suggest that headcovering among Jewish women was of eastern origin and only came to be applied with particular stringency by about the third century A.D.

Most assumptions about Diaspora Judaism appear to be based on rabbinical writings which cannot be dated any earlier than the close of the first Christian century, and it is untenable that whatever the Mishnah regards as traditional Jewish practice was of necessity in vogue in the first century. It is likely that in North Africa during the time of Tertullian veiling was strictly a Jewish custom, and still developing, and Jewesses were conspicuous on the streets because they wore veils. But there is reason to believe that even there, veils were removed upon entering the synagogue.[40] Therefore it can hardly be stated that Jewish customs would have compelled Paul to enjoin such a practice as veiling the head in worship. It simply makes no sense.

Concerning headcoverings for men there is even less harmony between Jewish custom and traditional views of I Corinthians 11. The Law of Moses provided for an elaborate headdress for the high priest, a miter of linen with gold engravings, and also elaborate bonnets for the other priests.[41] But there is nothing else in the Old Testament to elucidate this matter, particularly to suggest that a man should not cover his head in prayer.

Somewhere in history a custom arose requiring Jewish males to cover their heads with a tallith, a fringed shawl, when praying. And in more recent times a cap called a yarmulke came to be worn in all religious devotions, particularly reading the Torah. But there is no evidence that either of these customs dates from as early as the first Christian century. According to Strack and Billerbeck the tallith did not begin till at least the fourth century, and the precise nature of the covering is made questionable by the implication in the Babylonian Talmud that such was accomplished by drawing the mantle, or a portion of the outer garment, up over the back of the head.[42]

In either case, it appears that Judaism developed two customs concerning headcoverings, neither in harmony with common inferences from I Corinthians 11 and neither traceable to an early enough date so as to have a bearing on the problem addressed therein.

Among the Romans, customs concerning headcoverings are no more consistent than among the Jews. Plutarch states that normally Roman women covered their heads and men uncovered them when outdoors.[43] But remains of artwork representing several centuries depict only two basic styles for appearance in public; either a mantle draped over the back of the head, or the head left bare. One frieze of the Imperial family in the time of Augustus includes six women, five of whom are veiled. The head of Cleopatra, in a portrait found at Cherchel, Algeria, is veiled as is the statue of Livia, wife of Augustus, found in the villa of the Mysteries in Pompeii.[44] Some have suggested that priestesses also customarily wore a headcovering, but at least in the mystery cult of Dionysius around 50 B.C. priestesses went bareheaded, with the hair parted in the middle and tied back. The fresco of the Rape of Europa, also from Pompeii, depicts three bareheaded women standing and Europa seated on a bull. Europa is bare-breasted, but with a drape pulled up to the top of her head covering her back.[45] The majority of extant portraits and statues depict Roman women, whether married or single, at home, at the markets, at study, or in religious meditation, bareheaded. Of course, it is quite possible that all such artwork is fashioned according to models whose dress and posture were not typical of the period.

Men seem to have been bareheaded in most activities, but also contrary to the custom implied in I Corinthians 11 Roman men generally wore a mantle in worship and on solemn occasions. The heads of Agrippa and Augustus are shown to be veiled in ritual processions. Virgil makes reference to heads being shrouded before the altar with a Phrygian vestment,[46] and both Plutarch and Seneca indicate that this practice was customary at sacrifices.[47]

Headcovering was also known in Greece, and the extreme seclusion of wives in the classical period is common knowledge among historians. Various writers speak in detail concerning the veils which Greek women were expected to wear. Dio Chrysostom, who flourished at the close of the first century A.D., speaks of a common convention regarding feminine attire which, he explains, prescribes that women could be so dressed and should so deport themselves when in the street that nobody could see any part of them, neither of the face nor the rest of the body, and that they themselves might not see anything off the road. The same writer describes the veil worn by women in Tarsus and Thebes as covering the whole face except the eyes, the Plutarch indicates that the motive behind veiling was to hide the husband's possession from the gaze of other men. Concerning the Spartans he stated: "When someone inquired why they took their girls into public places unveiled, but their married women veiled, he said: 'Because the girls have to find husbands, and the married women have to keep those who have them.'"[48]

While the testimony of such notable writers seems convincing enough, and is in complete agreement with the general picture of the secluded lives of Greek women described earlier, the written testimony from Classical Greece is not supported by artistic relics from the same period. A great number of women are illustrated with a portion of the *himation* draped over the back of the head, but the prevailing style seems to have been an unveiled head with the hair plaited and pinned up in back.

Concerning veiling in worship, Macrobius says that both men and women prayed bareheaded.[49] The inscription of Andania gives an exact description of women taking part in a religious procession with no headcovering being mentioned, and the regulations for the cultic order of Lycosma actually prohibited the wearing of veils.[50] It is extremely unfortunate that no artifacts from Corinth have been discovered which might offer assistance in this regard. In view of the great variety in hairstyles, dress and headcoverings all over the ancient world, it is impossible to state with certainty anything concerning the significance of headcoverings in worship in this one city. But the fact that Corinth was known for vice and immorality might suggest that such conservative customs as veiling, as a symbol of purity or fidelity in marriage, may have been abandoned. On the other hand, it may have been that those of a stricter morality saw fit to dissociate themselves from their corrupt environment through a more conservative and symbolic dress code. But there is nothing in either Greek, Roman or Jewish culture which would have necessitated commanding Christian women to veil themselves in worship.

Symbolism in Hairstyles

Paul says as much, if not more, in this passage about the significance of appropriate hairstyles as he says concerning a headcovering. But his implications on this topic are easily misunderstood.

What does nature teach about hair length? The Greek term *phusis* has been understood variously by scholars. Some take it to refer to the laws governing physical creation, suggesting that whatever Mother Nature instructs should be considered the design and will of God. Others understand the term to refer to the general notion people have by reason of common sense. But most recognize that common sense has little to do with cultural traits, and certainly plays no significant role in most religious beliefs.

Koster is probably correct in stating that Paul used the term "nature" in much the same way as was common to the Greek diatribe, using Greek custom as evidence of what is essentially and naturally correct.[51] In Romans 2:14 Paul reflects upon certain nations doing by nature what is contained in the Law of Moses, without knowledge of it. But what happened to be natural and logical for them was not so of most other nations. In fact, it seems that a principal point made by Paul in his letters is that doing what is right is not necessarily, perhaps seldom ever, human nature. This suggests that Paul's appeal to nature, whatever he meant by it, has no theological significance but simply draws upon common ethnocentrism to add weight to his argument.

Yet it is precisely this interpretive approach which has prevailed through the centuries concerning this passage. Tertullian wrote:

> If it is shameful for a woman to be shaven or shorn, of course it is for a virgin. Hence, let the world, the rival of God, see to it if it asserts that

close cut hair is graceful to a virgin in like manner as that flowing hair
is to a boy.[52]

Although countless commentators and exegetes have so asserted, it
cannot be stated that nature, whether viewed as biological law, innate
human tendency or social pattern, suggests it shameful for men to have
long hair and for women to have shorn hair.

A careful study of hairstyles throughout history reveals nothing to
suggest that long hair is naturally shameful to men. Among many African
tribes hair length is hardly a factor in either hierarchy, beauty or sex
distinction, because by nature it does not grow long in either males or
females. In other cultures, such as Chinese, Persian, Tibetan and various
Indian cultures of North and South America, long hair styles have been
worn with great pride for centuries. In ancient Sumer, Babylonia, Egypt,
Assyria and Israel, hairstyles would clearly deny the idea of customary
shame associated with long hair in men. Even in Greece from the earliest
traceable history to the beginning of the classical age men wore their hair
shoulder length or longer. As modern research on hair has developed,
previously held theories about the natural difference in hair growth
between the two sexes have been abandoned, so that no legitimate claim
can be made that nature teaches anything of religious significance about
hairstyles in men or women.

What does nature teach about shaven and shorn women? It can be
truthfully stated that in most cultures long hair in women has been a point
of beauty, with a few exceptions. During certain periods of Egyptian
history both men and women shaved their heads, wearing wigs when going
outdoors. But in the eighteenth dynasty it became fashionable even for
women to go about in public with exposed and shaved heads. Hebrew
women, on the other hand, were expected to have long hair which would
only be cut to symbolize deep mourning or degradation, or perhaps to complete a solemn vow.[53]

It is quite reasonable to accept, however, that any woman of Paul's
day would have felt degraded if for some reason her hair were cut short,
or perhaps her head shaved, against her will. In this regard a question arises
as to why it might be a shameful thing, and why Paul draws this point into
the discussion.

Numerous commentators have suggested that prostitutes of various
types were identified by their shaved or shorn heads, but neither art
nor literature from relevant ancient cultures offers any evidence to this
effect.

However, there are certain indications that adulteresses might have
their hair cut as a public mark of guilt and shame. Tacitus records that
among the Germans the husband of an adulterous wife would cut off her

hair, strip her naked and drive her from his house.[54] Menander describes in one of his comedies the outrage done to a girl by a jealous lover who cut her hair short. Athenaeus refers to the cutting of a woman's hair as a gross insult, and Aristophanes, in reference to the mother of unworthy children, says: "Crop her hair and seat her lowly; brand her with the marks of shame."[55]

It is likely that Paul's reference had a special significance in his own day, which is born out by the terminology he selects.[56]

The verb *gzuran* means "to shave," as with a razor, and appears frequently in classical Greek literature in reference to shaving the face, the head or the entire body. The term may have been used only with regard to the shaving of the chin in light of Lucian's declaration that such action was unnatural for a woman and the statement of Epictetus that the hair of the chin is God-given to distinguish between male and female.[57] The word *keirein* means "to cut," "to shear," or "to clip short" the hair of the head, and was employed to describe the customary dressing of a man's hair, but not that of a women. A.T. Robertson says that the two imperatives used by Paul are best translated with a persuasive middle, so that the injunction would read: "Let her then have herself shorn . . . and shaven."[58] The expression "shave and shear" was no doubt a common barbering term in the Greco-Roman world, used strictly with reference to the daily grooming of men.

The women in the Corinthian church were clearly violating the standards of propriety, and in some fashion displaying their disregard for custom and for the authority of their husbands. Therefore Paul chided: "If you want to be equal with the men, then you may as well start shaving and get your hair cut so you can look like them. But if you feel that such actions would be degrading, then retain the customary symbols of femininity and subjection."

An Alternative to the Veil Theory

A number of inconsistencies arise in the traditional interpretation of I Corinthians 11:2–16 as dealing with the necessity of a veil for Christian women in worship. The language is uncertain when the simple term *kalumma* could have been employed repeatedly by Paul had he the traditional veil in mind. The customs among the Jews, Greeks and Romans concerning the wearing of headcoverings were not such as would necessitate such a ruling, especially when considering the various social liberties which early Christians enjoyed through freedom in Christ. And the appeal to "nature" carries little weight beyond the expectations or norms of any given society.

For these reasons various scholars have abandoned the traditional veil theory first propounded by Tertullian in favor of some approach which places less emphasis on the idea of symbolic modesty in worship. If it cannot be established that veiling in public or in worship was a custom in first-century Corinth, then there is no basis for such a doctrine.

Paul's mention of angels is also puzzling. Theologically, the idea of angels being embarrassed by a woman praying unveiled, or that she might be in any way more visible to angels while praying than at any other time, is quite ludicrous. Likewise the possibility of angels being tempted to lust by a woman praying without proper attire is untenable. Yet, it is possible that such was a common belief, at least among the Jews, and either Paul also believed it or simply drew from it for added argumentative weight. The legend of an angel periodically troubling the water at Bethesda (John 5:4) is recorded with no attempt at refutation, either by Jesus or the writer. Yet it is absurd to think that such really occurred.

The first step toward a more acceptable interpretation of the passage is taken by a few scholars who recognize that Paul's primary concern is with husband-wife relationships, and who therefore determine the headcovering in question as symbolic of the authority of the husband over the wife. This approach suggests that the Corinthian wives, particularly those who were prophetesses, were worshipping without veils to indicate their spiritual liberation and equality through Christ.[59] But in so doing they symbolically implied infidelity and unchastity and so brought shame upon their husbands. A variation of this approach is suggested by Isaksson, who interprets the "authority on her head" of verse 10 as a veil worn by prophetesses to signify their right to speak in a public assembly.[60] But it still remains doubtful whether the symbolism attached to the veil by the above theories ever existed, and whether it would have warranted such a treatment by Paul.

A newer theory, proposed by James Hurley, is far more plausible than any other proposition to date, yet it appears to have little scholastic acceptance.[61] Hurley contends that nowhere in the passage is there any suggestion of the need for a veil, a prayer shawl, or any artificial headcovering except verse 15, and that Paul's point is that woman's hair satisfies the need. Further, he suggests that Paul's introductory phrase "having something down from the head," was understood by the Corinthians to relate to hair, and not to an artificial headcovering. On the basis of several Septuagint passages Hurley contends that Paul's term "uncovered" was a common expression for having "loose flowing hair," while "covered" meant, at least with regards to women, having the hair pinned up in a bun or chiton.[62] The problem at Corinth, therefore, was that certain married women who had been endowed with the gift of prophecy had decided that their charismatic office combined with liberty in Christ freed them from social and legal subordination to their husbands. Therefore, in a display of liberation they let down their hair, as if they were single and under the authority of no man. It is for this reason that in the Greco-Roman world characteristically married women kept their hair pinned up, while single girls could wear their hair loose. Especially on her wedding day a virgin appeared with loose flowing locks to symbolize her innocence and freedom.

If Hurley's theory is correct, then Paul's approach to the problem becomes clear. Just as it would be unnatural and out of character for a man of his day to have his hair "pinned up," so would it be out of character for a Christian wife to symbolically deny her role of submission to her husband by "letting her hair down" in public. In addition, if Hurley's theory is correct the many classical references to covering the head might take on a new meaning, a possibility which is not without scholastic consideration. Clement of Alexandria stated:

> It is enough for women to protect their locks, and bind their hair simply along the neck with a plain hair pin, nourishing chaste locks with simple care to true beauty.[63]

Billerbeck, in a treatment of the dress codes of Judaism, suggests that for a woman to show herself to another man with her hair loose, or to allow another man to "uncover" her head, was flagrant violation of the husband's rights, an insult to her marriage, and the first step toward committing adultery.[64]

It is highly unlikely that the Apostle Paul required the wearing of veils by Christian women in worship, or that special headcoverings were required of prophetesses to signify their authority to speak publicly. But it is possible that various customs, including that style of veil required of Arab women, derived the concept of a sign of authority, meaning the subjection of the woman to some male's authority, from the same early basic idea as that referred to by Paul. The Arabic term for veil, *shultana*, is from the same root as the term "Sultan," meaning "ruler" or "authority."

Whether the subject of I Corinthians 11:2–14 is determined to be headcoverings or hairstyle, the principal point is that men and women should dress and act in accordance with propriety and social expectations as regards the roles distinguished by sex. And it is the subordinate position of the wife to her husband, which was strongly in force in all the cultures of Paul's day to which he addresses these stern admonitions.

VI. GENERAL CONDUCT

Suffice it to say that the general deportment of women in the early church was expected to be such that would promote peace and harmony with the body, and would exemplify godliness to those outside the faith.

Cullmann reiterates the feeling of both Overbeck and Schweitzer that early
Christians were motivated by an ardent expectation of the end.[65] They had
little time to waste on frivolities, but concentrated on preaching the Gospel,
both publicly and within the framework of daily activities. But they were
not so blinded by zeal for the Parousia as to lose sight of the fact that they
lived in a pagan world and were bound to live their convictions endeavor-
ing to peacefully influence others to accept their faith. While Christian men
and women were convinced that they were spiritually segregated from the
world, they recognized that they still had to buy meat from the local butch-
ers, comply with state laws, and rub shoulders with pagans in the streets
and markets. They were in the world, but not of the world. Therefore, their
pattern of living needed to be exemplary of godliness, purity and love, even
to the point of sacrificing personal liberties and enduring affliction
wrongfully for the sake of winning others to Jesus Christ.

Perhaps the finest summary of the ideal conduct of a Christian woman
is the conclusion to Paul's mention of adorning in I Timothy 2:9–10. Here
the apostle's desire is that women adorn themselves, not in braids, gold,
pearls and expensive clothing, "but as is proper for women who profess
God-fearing, by means of good works." Such good works are, of course,
the subject of much of New Testament instruction, and whatever practical
admonitions to godliness may be directed to a general audience certainly
apply to women as well as men. In the words of Hendriksen, "Divine grace
brings into existence the tree of faith on which these good works grow as
so many fruits."[66] Making an effort to do good and to be good is an essential
characteristic of those who follow in the footsteps of Jesus, who said, "Let
your light so shine before men that they may see your good works, and
glorify your Father which is in heaven."[67] Peter, in a similar fashion, con-
trasts the glamor of worldly women with daughters of God whose adorning
should be

> . . . the hidden man of the heart with the imperishable jewel of a meek
> and quiet spirit which in the sight of God is very precious.[68]

An adequate treatment of the godly conduct of a Christian woman would
require a discussion of the major part of the didactic material in the New
Testament, but the general features can be sketched in brief:

1. She must be a good wife, in subjection to her husband (Titus 2:4;
Ephesians 5:22, 33; I Corinthians 7:3ff.).

2. She must be a good mother to her children (Titus 2:4).

3. She must be discreet and chaste in behavior.

4. She must avoid the temptation of gossip, slander, backbiting and
the like (I Timothy 3:11).

5. She must be industrious in keeping the home (I Timothy 5:13).

6. She must be modest and discreet in dress (I Peter 3:3–4; I Timothy 2:9–10).

7. She must minister to sick, needy, imprisoned, and unfortunate in every avenue of charity (Acts 9:36).

8. She must be hospitable to strangers (Titus 2:3–6; I Timothy 5:10; Acts 16:15).

9. She must be quiet and unobtrusive.

10. She must be a student of the word of God, which is the personal responsibility of every Christian.

11. She must instruct others by every acceptable means (Acts 18:26; II Timothy 1:5; 3:4, 15).

12. She must endure affliction patiently (I Peter 2:18–3:2).

Church fathers after the first century were inclined to be more specific in dictating what kinds of activities the Christian should avoid, identifying forms of entertainment such as the games, theater, and the like. The *Apostolic Constitutions* make mention of the undesirable character of brawling women, and those who would go to the bath houses along with men.[69]

But in general New Testament writers deal with principles, leaving it to each generation of believers to make application in their own contexts. Dwight Pratt sees early Christian women as conspicuous in history for "maternal love, spiritual devotion and fidelity in teaching the word of God." He says:

> They exchanged the temples, theaters, and festivals of paganism for the home, labored with their hands, cared for their husbands and children, graciously dispensed Christian hospitality, nourished their spiritual life in the worship service and sacraments of the church, and in loving ministries to the sick.... That they were among the most conspicuous examples of the transforming power of Christianity is manifest from the admiration and astonishment of the pagan Libanius who exclaimed, "what women these Christians have!"[70]

6. Equality in Christ

In Galatians 3:28 Paul declares: "there can be neither Jew nor Greek, there can be neither bond nor free, there can be neither male nor female; for you are all one in Christ Jesus." This proclamation of freedom and equality is the key text for a summary of the New Testament position on the status of women. Paul here draws upon three critical areas of social stratification to illustrate the objective of the gospel and the nature of the kingdom of God. And it is in this triad that practical theology with regard to the place of women in the church finds its critical moment.

Having considered the attitude of Christ toward women and the somewhat elevated status of women in the early church as compared to earlier and contemporary history, the natural conclusion is that social equity between the sexes is one of the underlying objectives of Christianity. But the restrictions placed upon women by Paul, and by other New Testament writers to a lesser degree, become a hermeneutical stumbling block. Also somewhat paradoxical is the fact that the New Testament remains dominated by males: the Messiah, the apostles, the seven "deacons" of Acts 6, scores of evangelists, elders and deacons in countless churches of the first century. While evidence is strong that women filled prominent roles in many churches and that they exercised various charismatic gifts, there were clearly certain forces at work during that era which seemed designed to control and suppress any nontraditional trends in this regard.

Admittedly, to come to some degree of understanding of the cultural backgrounds which relate to the New Testament and the status of women is still not to explain the apparent discrepancies in doctrine, nor to resolve all the difficulties which arise in applying those teachings to a modern context. Can women rejoice triumphantly in response to their social liberation through Christ, or must they as his disciples resign themselves to the fact that the New Testament simply reiterates the cultural norms and traditions which have held them in subjection throughout history? Does Paul's alleged "emancipation proclamation" grant to Christian women the right to positions of leadership in the church, including that of evangelist, deacon and elder (or pastor, priest, bishop — whatever terms are appropriate), or must they face roles of subjection and subordination, perhaps with even fewer opportunities for service and leadership than their first-century sisters? These are the practical considerations with which many church people are concerned.

However, the practical application of exegetical and historical discoveries, especially if it involves change in established religious traditions, is never a simple task. Iconoclasts generally face ostracism by the establishment and often by their peers. But even when attempts are made to maintain harmonious relationships while change is brought about slowly, confrontation often is forced by the incompatibility of ideology and philosophy. Concerning this very difficulty Madeleine Boucher writes:

> Theologians are often led to fresh insights by the new factors operating in their own time, especially intellectual and social factors. Then, because they stand in the Judaio-Christian tradition, they turn to the Bible in search of texts with which to undergird these new insights. Yet, because they are seeking to answer contemporary questions, questions unknown to the biblical writers, they sometimes interpret the biblical texts in a way which is more true to contemporary thought than to the thought of the biblical writers. The recent discussion of the place of women in the church is an example. As said above, modern man, as a result of numerous and complex factors operating in the last three centuries, is no longer able to hold an abstract ideology of equality while refusing to translate it into practical terms.... Thus, a study of the New Testament teaching on the role of women leads finally to one of the important questions of theology today, that of the relationship between contemporary theology, on the one hand, and an authoritative Bible on the other hand.[1]

This observation helps explain why scholars tend to follow one of two divergent paths of interpretation concerning Galatians 3:28. This passage, with all its ramifications, is a pivotal point in practical theology and church doctrine with regard to the status of women.

I. SPIRITUAL EQUALITY ONLY

On one side of the fence are those who feel compelled to uphold the traditional position that male dominance, at least in the home and in church liturgy, is a divinely ordained pattern for all believers everywhere. Following a fundamental approach to this and related passages, advocates of this position might interpret Galatians 3:28 in the following fashion.

There can be little doubt that Paul was a zealous advocate of personal liberty. In the words of Caird, freedom in Jesus Christ is "one of the

inseparable corollaries of his [Paul's] doctrine of justification by faith."[2]
This in fact is the primary thrust of his letter to the Galatians, in which the
apostle compares legalistic Judaism to Hagar, a bondwoman rearing
enslaved children, while Christianity, the heavenly Jerusalem and covenant
of faith, corresponds to Sarah, the true wife, whose children are free.[3]

But the liberty of which Paul speaks is spiritual, not legal, political or
social. Caird continues:

> Christian liberty is, in the first instance, an unearned access to God,
> an emancipation from the shackles of the past, from the endictment of
> a guilty conscience, from the inner tensions between duty and inclina-
> tion, from the divisive claims of conflicting loyalties, from the unremit-
> ting demands of merit.[4]

The immediate context of Paul's statement is the reconciliation of Jew and
Gentile to God through a spiritual body, and the mention of slaves and
women is merely an extension of the same theme. Zerbst is representative
of those scholars who contend that Paul is concerned only with the spiritual
value of people to God, declaring his accessibility to everyone regardless
of social status:

> The realm has nothing to do either with the body or external forms of
> human society, but is wholly of a spiritual nature. . . . He [Paul] does not
> . . . destroy the civil order or do away with the gradation of rank,
> without which human society cannot exist.[5]

If this is indeed what Paul was saying then he would have had in mind
the mistaken belief among mány Jewish Christians that the Messianic
kingdom essentially excluded Gentiles unless they first avowed allegiance
to the Law of Moses. It might have application also to any converts of
Roman background who might be inclined to discriminate against those of
a non-citizen class. In either case, the apostle was concerned for their
awareness that all nations, all classes and both sexes have equal opportunity to serve God and find spiritual harmony with him.[6] In this sense,
according to another New Testament writer, Christianity equalizes the rich
and poor in the eyes of God since he does not measure spiritual relationships in terms of material wealth.[7]

Naturally these principles of spiritual equality should have both personal and social implications, but only to the extent of expressions of love,
compassion and fellowship in the church. They do not eradicate essential
forms of social stratification. No New Testament writer overtly denounces
slavery or any other form of social discrimination. It is certain that masters
and slaves shared in the early Christian community, but as in the case of
Paul's letter to Philemon there is no suggestion of dissolving those aspects

of inequity essential to the economy of the day. Instead inspired writers as a whole encouraged all parties to carry out the obligations of their status in the spirit of Christ.[8] Likewise the political hierarchy of the Roman Empire, with its technical distinction between slave and free classes and its essentially anti–Christian character, was to be honored and supported by all believers.[9]

Furthermore, even if it could be conceded that Paul's statement has some social implications there is still a striking contrast between class distinctions and those factors which distinguish male and female and the roles they are to play in marriage. God did not create mankind slave and free, rich and poor, nor did he assign to various groups the traits which tend to generate discrimination and exclusiveness. He did, however, create male and female and assign them distinct roles in marriage. Burton, advocating this line of interpretation, takes note of the "ineradicable distinction of sex," concluding that the passage has nothing to do directly with the practical merging of nationalities, annulling class distinctions or abolition of slavery.[10] Chadwick also sees Paul's words as the offer of moral choice and the responsibility of spiritual behavior, but not a program of political emancipation. The role of the husband and wife, he says, stays the same by God's authoritative design.[11] There are certain social distinctions which are inevitable in any culture. There will always be leaders and followers, teachers and pupils, rich and poor, employer and employee, governor and citizen; there will always be male and female. The New Testament does not instruct that such social distinctions are to be disregarded by Christians, or even that such should not persist within the body of believers, but that these standards have nothing to do with salvation or quality of service in the kingdom of God. Everyone can have a place of dignity and importance as a member of the body of Christ, even a Gentile, a slave and a woman.

II. COMPLETE SOCIAL LIBERATION

In contrast with the traditional line of reasoning, those scholars representing a broader perspective concerning the Gospel are inclined to see Galatians 3:28 as a statement of the ideal attainable if and when the principles of the Gospel penetrate the human heart, find a foothold in society and attain their objectives in socially meaningful ways. In simpler terms it means that the Gospel is a declaration of dignity and equality for all.[12]

The first objection to the traditional view is that it renders Galatians 3:28 meaningless, even in spiritual terms. In almost every religion of the ancient world, including Judaism, women enjoyed the same status as men when considered from the standpoint of blessings received from and relationship to their deities. As was the case with Israel, many cults were nationalistic and no individual could be thought of as having a greater or lesser degree of spiritual importance than anyone else, except of course the priests and prophets. But invariably it was the outward form of spiritual expression which discriminated against women; the exclusion from certain rituals, along with the ceremonial encumbrances and traditional taboos which made the lot of women unbearable. And, according to Paul, it was this useless body of tradition from which Jews could be freed through the sacrifice of Jesus Christ. If acknowledgement by God as the spiritual equal of men was her only benefit, a Jewess would have little to gain by converting to Christianity. According to the *Genesis Rabbah*, rabbis taught that on a spiritual plane all are equal, whether rich or poor, slave or free, man or woman. Furthermore, when considering the fact that apart from Christ, according to Romans 3:9, Jew and Gentile alike were under sin there is no change in lateral relationship when the two are brought together in Christianity. They are equal in condemnation and equal in salvation. The same is true of men and women. If the equalizing force of Christ pertains only to spiritual relationships then it has no practical merits at all in terms of human conduct and social relationships.

A further objection to the traditional line of reasoning is that it tends to create a monstrous contradiction between what is commonly recognized as Christian ideology and actual New Testament doctrine. While New Testament writers, and more significantly Jesus himself, encourage the support of government officials, even if they happen to be evil and their form of rule tyrannical, the underlying principles of New Testament theology clearly oppose tyranny. While inspired writers encourage slaves to submit to their masters and masters are instructed to treat slaves fairly, which in technical terms must be taken as supportive of slavery, the underlying principles of love, mercy, equity and justice clearly oppose slavery. In time, where these concepts would permeate society they would gradually eliminate various forms of social injustice in spite of the fact that fundamentally the New Testament teaches Christians to tolerate and submit to the less desirable social order.

Further evidence that Paul had more in mind than mere spiritual status is the practical and social implications of Christianity to Jews and Gentiles. The three pairs mentioned in Galatians 3:28 denote the three deepest divisions which split society in the first century, and were the three specific classes mentioned in the Jewish morning prayer. Because of their understanding of the Law of Moses pious Jews held themselves apart from those of less desirable social strata, especially Gentiles. For this reason Jews converted to Christianity continued to be intolerant of Gentiles and found it difficult to have social and religious fellowship with them. Some attempted to impose on their Gentile brothers a few basic Jewish regulations, which in some way would satisfy their traditional prejudice. The Jerusalem Council of Acts 15 was conducted to deal with just such a problem, and in the end a few concessions were made to keep the peace till both groups could attain maturity and tolerance. But it seems that this was a major problem throughout the early church, and the Apostle Paul addressed himself at length to the concept of breaking down the dividing wall between ethnic groups so that believers could become a unified body. On at least one occasion Paul opposed Peter face to face when the latter revealed an unwholesome duplicity in refusing to eat with Gentile converts. His resistance to change, and that of Judaizers whom he supported, was contrary to the true meaning of the Gospel and served to quench the spirit of grace.

No doubt similar tension developed between members of different socio-economic strata. There was some consolation in knowing that God did not measure their spiritual worth in terms of material possessions. But writers such as James, John and Paul draw attention to the practical aspects of social inequity. From the outset wealthy Christians were encouraged to share their abundance with the poor, and to avoid discrimination against them in the affairs of the church. Likewise the poor were encouraged to maintain faith, and the lazy were admonished to work in order to have possessions with which to support their own relatives and to share with others who might have nothing.

It becomes evident that certain problems which existed in the first century would not find a practical solution till centuries later. This was clearly the case concerning slavery. Observing this anomaly, Stendahl asks, "Does the New Testament contain elements, glimpses, which point beyond and even against the prevailing view and practice of the New Testament church?" Stendahl's answer is a resounding "yes."[13] This means that while in principle the New Testament might oppose slavery, racism, tyranny and other forms of social injustice, it appears to advocate or at least tolerate such undesirable concepts in practice simply because the time had not come for their overthrow. This would take years, in fact centuries, of growth on the part of the church and of advancement of social mentality.

This seems to be the case concerning the status of women also. In practical terms the various restrictions placed upon women in the early Christian community were necessitated by social and cultural pressures, but were not intended as universal church dogma. In Galatians 3:28 the Apostle Paul reveals the ultimate, the ideal, in Christian objectives, setting aside in theory all practical rules of subordination and declaring the freedom of all subjected classes, slaves, Gentiles and women, from social discrimination. Like the prophetic view of the kingdom as a people who would beat swords into plowshares and never lift up sword against each other again,[14] so this concept stretches out to the fullest practical realization of the ideal. It presupposes maturity on the part of all believers, and a social environment tolerant of Christian ideals. After twenty centuries this still has not occurred in its fullest sense. But the beauty lies in its potential and in its practical application even in limited contexts. The implications of all this to believers of that era as well as the present are summarized by Glen:

> Both Jew and Gentile were to be reconciled in their actual outward relationships as well as in spirit and mind. . . . The Gospel is the power that shattered and continues to shatter slavery, not only as a spiritual and mental form of bondage, but as an institution; no less that form of slavery, the formal institution of subordination of women to men.[15]

If therefore Paul's words do not suggest the practical emancipation of women, to be evidenced first in the role of women in the church and second in the sphere of social relationships, then they have no meaning at all.

III. SEEDS OF CHANGE

According to Romans 12:1-2, Christians should resist conformity with the standards set by the world, at least where those standards are inferior to the godly principles set forth in the New Testament. Where no ethical principle is at stake and where institutional law or social expediency requires, conformity is in fact the right course. But as a general rule Christians march to a different drummer and look beyond mere social customs and standards for behavioral guidance. They are to be kind, considerate, polite, loving, forgiving, compassionate, merciful, tolerant, understanding and cooperative even when the world is not. They seek to maintain self-control when others are self-indulgent; to be at peace when others are at war; to hold their tongues when others are vile; to minister to those whom the world might reject; to do good and support what is intrinsically right even in face of mockery and alienation.

This means that in practical relationships Christians will insist on commonality of fellowship across social, economic and racial barriers even when society has not become so tolerant. It means that Christians should represent the avant-garde in subtle and peaceful social change in an upward direction, based on the elevated concepts revealed in the mind and person of Jesus Christ. It means that while Christians cannot force changes in society, they can lead society in a positive direction by exemplifying elevated standards in their own homes, in the church and in daily contact with people of the world. They should be the first to understand and practice the principles of their faith, not the last.

Problems surrounding the social and religious status of women were clearly prominent in the early Christian era. The record of apostolic activities in Acts indicates that from the start women were converting to

Christianity in great numbers, as they were to many of the mystery religions which had become so popular in the Mediterranean world. Part of the appeal of Christianity, no doubt, was the absence of discrimination. In the early church women were involved in every aspect of community life such as giving to the poor, expressing hospitality, participating in fellowship meals, the study and discussions of holy scriptures, singing, prayer, communion, dialogue in the church assembly and proclaiming the Gospel to their community.

But something happened in various churches about which we can only speculate. Perhaps all these changes were too dramatic and happened too quickly. Perhaps they were somewhat ahead of their time. This is not difficult to imagine, since even though God deemed the time right for the Messiah the Jews as a whole were ready neither for him nor his kingdom. In any case, the tension created by the essential liberties afforded women in churches such as Corinth necessitated certain forms of control and restraint purely because of the difficulties of change, at least the nature of change demanded by Christianity. The cost of discipleship was great, not just in terms of sacrificing material possessions, alienation by family and friends or the threat of physical persecution, but in radical adjustments of deep-seated attitudes, values and world perspective. Such was the impact of Jesus Christ on those who elected to follow him.

In order to preserve harmony among believers and to protect their positive influence in the community, certain concessions had to be made. Caird appropriately lauds the Apostle Paul as a champion of female liberty in spite of his sensible compliance with social expediency:

> Some of Paul's teaching on the position of women appears to us out of date only because he addressed himself to the social condition of his own day, and because we sometimes imperfectly understand the problems with which he had to deal.[16]

The possibility of certain concessions and occasional accommodative language should not be difficult for any student of the Bible to accept. Jesus himself described the Mosaic teaching on divorce as a concession to the hardness of the human heart. But from the very beginning this was considerably less than ideal.[17] The Old Testament is pregnant with examples of substandard behavior on the part of judges, kings and prophets, much of which is passed over with no hint of God's displeasure. The Law of Moses itself is to be seen by the Christian as an inadequate and inferior substitute for the ideal covenant enacted through the ministry of Jesus Christ.

Clearly Pauline teaching on master and slave relationships was a concession to inferior and undesirable social conditions, which teaching we

today apply to employer and employee relationships with little consideration of the changes since Paul's day. Likewise the advice sent by the
Jerusalem Council of Acts 15 to the Gentile Christians in Antioch was
largely a matter of concession to the narrowmindedness of Jewish Christians who had not yet grown to the point of relinquishing the Law of Moses
and forcing themselves to accept uncircumcised Gentiles, with all their
disgusting eating habits, as equals in the daily communal affairs of the
church. But all these concessions were simply to grant the church and the
world time to grow.

The same is true concerning the New Testament teaching on the status
of women. But on this issue change has been far too slow. What had a striking and promising beginning at Pentecost and during the early days of
apostolic seems to have faded into cultural oblivion by the second century,
purely because of human stubbornness and pride.

There are ample indications that social changes of this sort were brew-
ing elsewhere in the world, even in Judaism around the time of Christ. For
example, a statement in the *Midrash* ascribed to Rabbi Akibah, around A.D.
135, reads: "I call heaven and earth to witness that whether Gentile or
Israelite, man or woman, slave or handmaid reads this verse, northward
before the Lord, the Holy One, blessed be he." And a quotation from the
Genesis Rabbah reads: "If a poor man says anything one pays little regard;
but if a rich man speaks immediately he is heard and listened to. Before
God, however, all are equal: men, women, slaves, poor and rich." And still
another, which demonstrates pointedly the changing attitudes toward
marital roles and the created order, reads:

> In the past Adam was created from dust and Eve was created from
> Adam; but henceforth it shall be 'in our image and after our likeness'
> (Genesis 1:26); neither man without the woman nor woman without
> man, and neither without Shekinah.[18]

While these teachings may have been understood to refer only to spiritual
status, as in the traditional interpretation of Galatians 3:28, they
nonetheless represent a broadening of perspective among Jewish rabbis
during the same general period in which Christianity was born.

When Jesus was questioned concerning his views on divorce and
remarriage he appealed to the creation narrative in Genesis, seemingly to
establish divine intention.[19] But it is noteworthy that he quoted part of the
former account in which the creation included both male and female, rather
than the Yahwist account which has Eve made from one of Adam's ribs.
He then picked up one verse from the second account, Genesis 2:24, to
make a practical point concerning the marital bond and the lasting union
between a man and woman if their relationship approaches the ideal. We

cannot say that Jesus rejected the other details as mythical, but he clearly avoided them. In keeping with his typical response to the plight of women Jesus gave no support to the traditions which contributed to female degradation. Paul, on the other hand, found reason to do so. In his first letter to Timothy he makes a special effort to point out that Adam was created first, and that it was Eve, Adam's refashioned rib bone, who fell to the temptation of Satan.[20] Of course, there are advocates of male dominance who defend Adam by arguing that he ate of the forbidden fruit only out of compassion, unwilling to let Eve bear the consequences of sin alone. But honesty compels us to acknowledge that males are in no way superior to females with regard to resistance to temptation. Males characteristically differ from females in various ways, and individuals all have their own personal strengths and weaknesses. But with regard to the general human inclination to sin, people are people.

Although to this point we have defended Pauline motives in placing restrictions on women in the church, it may be that in this passage the tension being experienced by Jewish society concerning the status of women is reflected in the contrast between Jesus and Paul. This would not be the first time that an apostle had difficulty breaking out of his traditional mentality and yielding to the spirit of the Gospel. Peter was very reluctant to accept Gentiles into fellowship in spite of his own role in initiating evangelism among them. But such inconsistencies are typical of human beings, regardless of their status, and the apostles were indeed human. Therefore, despite the foregoing arguments that Paul's restrictions on women might be seen strictly as transient concessions to inferior and essentially anti–Christian cultural norms, there is also the possibility that Paul struggled with personal prejudice as much as anyone else, and that his written suggestions on the status of women reflect more of his own thinking than divine inspiration. But the latter is thought to place excessive strain on conservative views of inspiration, and is quickly rejected in those circles as a solution to our immediate dilemma.

IV. EQUALITY IN HOME AND CHURCH

Passages like I Corinthians 11:3 and Ephesians 5:23, coupled with various instructions to wives concerning submission, have served through the years as ample basis for the perpetuation of the traditional marriage hierarchy. Bowing to the authority of holy writ, Christians generally maintain that the husband is the head over the wife and family and that God is displeased with any marital relationship not so structured.

However, looking at these passages from a fresh perspective, and indeed taking a second look at inspiration and the purpose of scripture to the lives of readers, the disillusioning mist of inconsistency begins to clear, and truths begin to appear which often escape the attention of those bound to a traditional modality.

One fresh approach to the two passages cited above involves an alternate interpretation of Paul's concept of headship. Traditionally this has been thought of as a metaphor for government, authority and superior rank. The husband has been understood to be the divinely ordained commanding officer of the family, making final decisions, approving all plans and activities and acting as spiritual mentor to both wife and children. Some have observed, however, that the concept of headship might refer to a relationship of unity and mutually supportive love rather than the authority of one entity over another. The husband is not to view the wife as a detached possession but an integral part of himself, sharing his burdens, feeling his pain, supporting his ambitions, enjoying his successes. She is one with him, and he therefore should love her as he loves and cares for his own body, feeling acute sensitivity and compassion for all her needs. With much the same force Peter writes that husbands should "treat their wives with consideration in their life together" (I Peter 3:7), in spite of their typically weaker bodies. The Christian doctrine of love must have an impact on marital relationships, just as it does on all other human relationships, eventually overpowering and replacing patterns rooted in pride, prejudice, selfishness and ego competition. The ideal marriage should be a relationship of balance, mutual respect, harmony and fulfillment, all springing from the fountain of sacrificial love. There is no place in such an elevated concept for a system which assigns rank and authority automatically on the basis of gender.

Since the New Testament treatment of the subordination of wives generally appears in the same context as the subjection of slaves to their masters and the like, it becomes clear that such forms of hierarchy reflect a stage of social and spiritual immaturity destined for collapse. They represent not only an inferior form of human relationship but also a transient form, dependent almost entirely upon the character and development of the societies in which they exist. While writers like Paul felt compelled to support these forms in their own day, they, like the Old Testament prophets, envisioned a time when superior standards would burgeon from the Gospel. To this end believers were urged to labor patiently, adopting the mind and attitude of Christ and maintaining persistent growth toward maturity.

This approach to Galatians 3:28 denounces all forms of social discrimination and inequity, including those against women in the home and in the church, even if Paul and his peers found it necessary to acquiesce in their own time as they did to slavery, tyranny and persecution. On a practical basis this sets aside the subordinate role of a wife to her husband and

establishes them as equal partners in marriage, with all duties and responsibilities to be arranged and agreed upon between them. The notion of
superiority, authority and lordship of husbands over their wives is clearly
antiquated and inferior, having no genuine support in the principles or
spirit of Christianity.

Furthermore, this approach would find authorization in divine principle for a female to hold any position of religious leadership for which she
may be deemed qualified by her peers, using the principles set forth in the
New Testament as guidelines for selection, training, ordination and nature
of duties and responsibilities.

V. COMING OF AGE

A few New Testament writers, Paul among them, foresaw a wave of
apostasy which would pose a far greater threat to the church than might
individual or cultural differences. Some of those forces were already at
work during the first century in the form of Gnosticism, Docetism and the
like. Christians were warned to be on guard and not permit such
movements to rob them of either their salvation or their liberty in Christ.
But many were swayed nevertheless. And one of the most tragic aspects of
this great departure from the faith was an anti-feminist movement among
churchmen of the second and third centuries which crippled for the next
fifteen hundred years the freedom and equality for women which was an
integral part of the Gospel message. During the period called the Dark
Ages, enlightenment and social advance, which otherwise might spring
naturally from evangelism, was actively thwarted by the orthodox church.
And not until the sixteenth-century Protestant Reformation was any significant progress made in relating the Gospel to the lives of ordinary people
or to significant areas of social injustice.

In Ephesians 4:11–16 the Apostle Paul looks longingly to the day when
the church would come of age, when its doctrine and its members would
display the kind of maturity that would radiate love to all the world by
ministering to human needs on both a spiritual and physical plane, and
which would demonstrate effectively the magnanimity of the spirit of
Christ by its positive impact on personal and social evils. But that maturity
has developed slowly, and the status of women is among the last socially
critical issues to be addressed meaningfully by Christian scholars and
churchmen, particularly among those of conservative and fundamentalist
leanings.

Perhaps the time has come for all believers to be, in the words of John
A.T. Robinson, "honest to God" about an entire range of significant questions which the traditional application of scripture has not addressed and

cannot address in a meaningful and sensible way. This demands that Christians rethink their position on the very nature of God, the manner and nature of biblical inspiration and the genuine message of the New Testament. And such rethinking demands that we overcome the nagging fear of losing sectarian identity and traditional heritage should such be found void of relevance or theological veracity. Any institution or body of doctrine established in an effort to restore or imitate the real thing, but which proves to be a dismal failure in spite of its claims to glory, is not worth preserving. Instead, it becomes a transient stepping-stone in the essential process of maturing.

Notes

1. Jesus and Women

[1]Luke 4:18-19; Isaiah 61:1ff.

[2]W. Rauschenbush, "Jesus the Builder of the New Society," *Great Lives Observed Jesus*, Hugh Anderson, editor (Englewood Cliffs NJ: Prentice Hall, 1967), p. 126; H.S. Vigeveno, *Jesus the Revolutionary* (Glendale CA: G/L Publications, reprinted 1972), pp. 5-12.

[3]Shailer Matthews, "Jesus' Philosophy of Social Progress," *Great Lives Observed Jesus*, p. 122; cf. Matthews, *The Social Teaching of Jesus, an Essay in Christian Sociology* (New York: Macmillan, 1897), pp. 191-197.

[4]Oscar Cullmann, *The Early Church*, A.J.B. Higgins, editor (London: SCM, 1956), p. 195.

[5]Bobby Lee Holley, "God's Design: Woman's Dignity," *Mission* III:10 (April, 1975), p. 294.

[6]Henri Daniel-Rops, *Jesus in His Time*, R.W. Millar, translator (London: Eyre and Spottiswoode, revised edition, 1956), p. 252.

[7]D.M. Pratt, "Women," *International Standard Bible Encyclopedia*, Vol. V (Grand Rapids MI: Eerdmans, reprinted 1955), p. 3102.

[8]Martin Dibelius, *Jesus* (London: SCM, 1939; English edition, 1963), p. 54.

[9]Marcello Craveri, *The Life of Jesus*, C.L. Markmann, translator (New York: Grove, 1967), pp. 9-10. Otto Hophan, *Maria* (Turin: Marietti, 1953), p. 51.

[10]Luke 1:27-38. Bultmann regards this and the parallel in Matthew 1:18-25 an adaptation from Hellenistic sources; see Rudolf Bultmann, *The History of the Synoptic Tradition*, John Marsh, translator (Oxford: Basil Blackwell, 1963, revised edition), p. 296.

[11]Luke 1:46-55. The speaker of the Magnificat is uncertain. Manuscript evidence is overwhelmingly in favor of Mary. Cf. B. Metzger, *A Textual Commentary on the Greek New Testament* (London: United Bible Societies, 1971), pp. 130-131. The hymn is closely modeled after the Song of Hanna (I Samuel 2:1-10) and neither Mary nor Elizabeth can be credited with its composition; cf. C.M. Connick, *Jesus, the Man, the Mission, and the Message* (Englewood Cliffs NJ: Prentice Hall, 1963), p. 104. The same is true of the Benedictus (Luke 1:68-79) attributed to Zechariah, which heralds the birth of the Messiah and in its present context is somewhat out of place.

[12]Matthew 1:20, 25; Isaiah 7:14. The "Virgin Birth" tradition is not without difficulties. Leaney argues that Luke's principal source for the Infancy Narrative was a tradition that Mary was already pregnant upon her encounter with the angel,

Joseph and Mary having cohabited since betrothal. The virginal conception was then a Christian notion which Luke incorporated into his narrative. See A.R.C. Leaney, *A Commentary on the Gospel According to St. Luke* (London: Adam and Charles Black, 1958), pp. 20–27. The theory, however, violates Jewish marriage customs. On the Virgin Birth see Connick and older works such as F.W. Farrar, *The Life of Christ* (New York: World, 1913, new edition 1965), pp. 1–8; James Orr, *The Virgin Birth of Christ* (New York: Scribner's, 1907); and W.C. Allen, "Matthew," *International Critical Commentary* (Edinburgh: T and T Clark, third edition, 1965), pp. 18–22.

[13]Luke 2:1–4. Connick, p. 106, doubts the plausibility of such a journey on grounds that a betrothed woman would not have been permitted to leave the home of her parents. A further problem is created by Luke's mention of Quirinius, the imperial legate in Syria-Cilicia between A.D. 6 and 9, in that the birth of Jesus took place at least ten years earlier. It is possible that Quirinius was legate twice, or that the census was inaugurated by Herod and completed a decade later in the time of Quirinius.

[14]For example Ambrose, Gregory of Nyssa, John Damascene, *et al.* A.J. Maas, "Virgin," *Catholic Encyclopedia*, Vol. XV (New York: Robert Appleton, 1912), p. 464H.

[15]Matthew 2:1–16; probably Babylonian astrologers or zoroastrian priests. That such magi should interpret the appearance of an astronomical phenomenon as indicative of the birth of a great prophet or prince is not unlikely. See Connick, p. 109; Allen, p. 14.

[16]The Slaughter of Innocents has no historical testimony outside of Matthew. Bultmann contends that the stories of the census, the shepherds, the magi and the slaughter of babies are all drawn from Hellenistic sources, and are woven into narrative form by the authors of Matthew and Luke for literary purposes. The birth of the Messiah in the circumstances portrayed by these two evangelists he considers untenable. (Bultmann, pp. 297–298.)

[17]Herod the Great died in 4 B.C.; cf. Matthew 2:14–23.

[18]Luke 2:19; cf. 2:51.

[19]Simeon's *Nunc Dimitis*, Luke 2:29–37. There is actually no clear authority for presenting the child in the temple; the account appears to imitate the presentation of Samuel, I Samuel 1:1–28. Bultmann sees parallels in the lives of numerous religious leaders and kings, e.g. Cyrus, Plutarch, Alexander the Great, Apollonius, and the Egyptian prince Si-Osire. Bultmann, pp. 300–301.

[20]Luke 2:46.

[21]Rudolf Bultmann, *The Gospel of John, a Commentary* , G.R. Beasley-Murray, translator (Oxford: Basil Blackwell, 1971 edition), p. 116.

[22]John 7:30, 8:20, 12:23, 13:1, 16:21, 17:1.

[23]Stoneware, as opposed to earthenware, did not contract Levitical impurity; cf. Leviticus 11:33; H.L. Strack and Paul Billerbeck, *Kommentar zum Neuen Testamentum aus Talmud und Midrash*, Vol. II (Munich: Beck, 1922, reprinted 1970), pp. 406ff; John's theme of water — 1:26, 3:5, 4:10, 6:53, 7:38. The writer is careful to note the capacity of each, "two to three measures," being one and a half Roman *amphorae*, or about nine gallons.

[24]John 2:11. For a thorough treatment of miracle itself, see Oscar Cullmann, *Early Christian Worship* (London: 1954), pp. 55, 71.

[25]Dodd calls the Cana Narrative "a naive tale about a marvel at a village wedding"; although he concludes that behind John there lies a tradition independent of the Synoptics, shaped in a Jewish-Christian environment, and still in touch with the

Palestinian synagogue before the rebellion of A.D. 66 (C.H. Dodd, *Historical Tradition in the Fourth Gospel* [Cambridge: Cambridge University Press, 1965], pp. 297, 315–321. Bultmann also denies the historicity of the incident, suggesting that it was taken over from heathen legend and ascribed to Jesus, (Bultmann, *Gospel of John*, p. 118.) Barrett, on the basis of legends concerning the transformation of water into wine by Dionysius, Philo's allegory of Melchizedek, and other parallels, regards it quite conceivable that the Cana miracle had a non–Christian origin. C.K. Barrett, *The Gospel According to John* (London: SPCK, 1955), p. 157. Cf. D.F. Strauss, *The Life of Jesus Critically Examined* (London: SCM, 1973), pp. 526–527.

[26]Raymond E. Brown, "Roles of Women in the Fourth Gospel," *Theological Studies* 36 (December, 1975), p. 689.

[27]Bernard is confident that an actual incident lies behind 2:1–11. J.H. Bernard, "Gospel According to St. John," *International Critical Commentary*, Vol. I (Edinburgh: T and T Clark, reprinted 1969), pp. clxxxiff 72–83.

[28]John 2:12; cf. Mark 2:1ff.

[29]Mark 3:31–35; cf. Matthew 12:46–50; Luke 8:19–21. The three Synoptic accounts of this incident are placed in different settings, however.

[30]Matthew 10:37; Luke 14:26; 18:29.

[31]Luke 11:27–28.

[32]John 19:25–27. The other writers, omitting the mother of Jesus, say that the women "stood afar off": Matthew 27:55; Mark 15:40; Luke 23:49. But even the Fourth Gospel avoids mentioning her name.

[33]Sychar, near the ancient site of Shechem, is thought to be the modern village of Belatah. The locality is approximately 1900 feet above sea level, on the ridge running from Mt. Ebal to Mt. Gerizim, and the well located there was dug by Jacob in a parcel of ground left as a legacy to Joseph (Genesis 33:19; 48:22). The same well, identified by Lebreton as the Moslem Bir Iaqub, is now sheltered by an abandoned Russian Orthodox church.

[34]John 4:1–45.

[35]D. Daube, "Jesus and the Samaritan Woman: The Meaning of *Sugchraomai*," *Journal of Biblical Literature* LXIX (1950), p. 137–147; *Mishnah* "Niddah" 4:1.

[36]Matthew 10:5.

[37]Bo Reike, *The Gospel of Luke*, R. Mackenzie, translator (Richmond: John Knox, 1962), p. 63; cf. Luke 9:52–56, 10:30ff., 16:16, Acts 1:8.

[38]Bultmann, *Gospel of John*, p. 180; W.F. Howard, "The Gospel According to John," *The Interpreter's Bible*, Vol. VIII, G.A. Buttrick, editor (New York: Abingdon, 1952), p. 525; C.K. Barrett, p. 197.

[39]Strauss, pp. 304–308; Craveri, p. 260; Dodd, pp. 315–321. Bultmann sees the Fourth Gospel as a product of a former Gnostic disciple, anxious to adapt gnosticism to Christianity, and edited later by an ecclesiastical redactor, (*Gospel of John*, pp. 1 ff.); Ernst Kasemann sees the Gospel in its present state as an attempt to replace primitive Christianity with Gnosticism, (Ernst Kasemann, *The Testament of Jesus* [1968]; Cullmann, however, sees the work as the earliest of the Gospels, though none were composed by an eye witness, and written by a community very much in touch with the historical Jesus and primitive Christianity (Oscar Cullmann, *The Johannine Circle*, John Bowden, translator [London: SCM, 1976], pp. 40–49, 97). Cf. Cullmann's preface (p. x) in which he explains his opposition to the Tubingen school; Robinson feels that John the son of Zebedee can be credited with the composition of the Fourth Gospel, with his disciples affixing the certificate in 21:24 (John A.T. Robinson, *Redating the New Testament* [London: SCM, 1976], p. 310);

cf. A.M. Hunter, *According to John* (London: SCM, 1968), pp. 3–10, for trends in scholastic views on the Fourth Gospel.

⁴⁰The pericope is absent from the major uncials and probably also from the oldest versions. No Greek church father before the twelfth century comments on the passage. In addition the passage interrupts the sequence of 7:52 and 8:12ff., plus it is recognized to be of a different style and vocabulary from the rest of the Fourth Gospel. Some ancient manuscripts insert it after 7:52, others after 7:44, 21:25 or after Luke 21:38. Cf. Metzger, pp. 219–221.

⁴¹Leviticus 20:10; Deuteronomy 22:23f.; *Mishnah* "Sanhedrin" 7:4, 11:1; "Makkoth" 1:1–10.

⁴²Luke 7:48–50.

⁴³Martha's name is derived from an Aramaic form not found in Hebrew meaning "lady" or "mistress." Three of the Gospels pinpoint a supper in Bethany at the house of Simon, with Martha serving the meal (John 12:1; Mark 14:3; Matthew 26:6), and for this reason some think Martha to have been the wife of Simon; others suggest that Simon was the father of Mary, Martha and Lazarus. Bultmann, *Gospel of John*, p. 414, fn. 7.

⁴⁴Luke 10:38–42.

⁴⁵Norval Geldenhuys, *Commentary on the Gospel of Luke* (Grand Rapids MI: Eerdmans, reprinted 1968), p. 317.

⁴⁶Matthew 6:33.

⁴⁷Leon Morris, *The Gospel According to John* (Grand Rapids MI; Eerdmans, 1965), pp. 533ff; Frederick L. Godet, *Commentary on the Gospel of John* (Grand Rapids MI: Zondervan, reprinted 1970), p. 184; B.F. Westcott, *The Gospel According to St. John* (Grand Rapids MI: Eerdmans, reprinted 1971), pp. 163–164.

⁴⁸The Synoptics do speak of Jesus as claiming to raise the dead (Matthew 11:5; Luke 7:22), and give two specific examples, the daughter of Jairus (Matthew 9:18ff.; Mark 5:22ff.; Luke 8:41ff.) and the son of the widow of Nain (Luke 7:11ff.).

⁴⁹John 12:1–9.

⁵⁰Matthew 16:16.

⁵¹John 12:1–9; Matthew 26:6–13; Mark 14:3–9.

⁵²Luke 7:36–50.

⁵³Luke 10:38–42; John 12:1–11.

⁵⁴Mark 5:25–34; Matthew 9:20–22; Luke 8:43–48.

⁵⁵Leviticus 15:25–28.

⁵⁶Letha Scanzoni and Nancy Hardesty, *All We're Meant to Be* (Waco TX: Word, 1974), p. 57.

⁵⁷Matthew 15:21–28; Mark 7:24–30.

⁵⁸A.B. Bruce, "The Synoptic Gospels," *The Expositor's Greek Testament*, Vol. I (Grand Rapids MI: Eerdmans, reprinted 1970), p. 216.

⁵⁹The story of the centurion, Matthew 8:10.

⁶⁰Centurion, Luke 7:9, Matthew 8:10; Syrophoenician woman, Matthew 15:28; four men carrying a paralytic, Matthew 9:2, Mark 2:5, Luke 5:20; woman with an issue of blood, Matthew 9:22, Mark 5:34, Luke 8:48; Bartimaeus and friend, Matthew 9:29, Mark 10:52, Luke 18:42; sinful woman who anointed Jesus, Luke 7:50; leper, Luke 17:19.

⁶¹Luke 13:10–17.

⁶²Geldenhuys, p. 375, fn. 1.

⁶³Donald Guthrie, *Jesus the Messiah* (Grand Rapids MI: Zondervan, 1972), p. 207.

⁶⁴Daniel-Rops, pp. 349–350; *Mishnah* "Shekalim," VI:5.

[65]Luke 21:1–4; Mark 12:41–44.

[66]*Mishnah* "Shekalim" I:5.

[67]The precise identity of some of the women is uncertain, but several facts are made clear by the following analysis of those present at three crucial events. Mary Magdalene is prominent, but Jesus' mother appears only in Fourth Gospel account of the crucifixion scene. Mary, wife of Cleopas, appears to be the sister of Jesus' mother, and also the mother of James the Less and Joses. Salome is the mother of James and John, and wife of Zebedee.

Crucifixion: Matthew 27:56 includes Mary Magdalene, and Mary the mother of Zebedee's children. Mark 15:40 mentions Mary Magdalene, Mary the mother of James the Less and Joses, and Salome (all looking from afar). John 19:25 mentions Jesus' mother, his mother's sister, Mary of Cleopas and Mary Magdalene.

Burial: Matthew 27:61 mentions Mary Magdalene, and the other Mary. Mark 15:47 mentions Mary Magdalene and Mary mother of Joses. Luke 23:55 says simply "the women."

Resurrection: Matthew 28:1 mentions Mary Magdalene and the other Mary. Mark 16:1 mentions Mary Magdalene, Mary mother of James, and Salome. Luke 24:10 mentions Mary Magdalene, Mary mother of James, Joanna and "others." John 20:1ff. mentions only Mary Magdalene.

[68]Daniel-Rops, p. 449.

[69]John 20:11–18. Note should be taken, however, that Mark 16:9 is the first verse of the spurious long ending of Mark, traceable to the early second century, but lacking in manuscript testimony.

[70]Craveri, p. 263.

[71]David Catchpole, "The Synoptic Divorce Material as a Traditio-Historical Problem," *Bulletin of the John Rylands University Library of Manchester*, 57:1 (Autumn, 1974), p. 93; B. Cohen, "Concerning Divorce in Jewish and Roman Law," *Proceedings of the American Academy for Jewish Research* XXI (1952), 3–34; See Above, pp. 133–134.

[72]Ecclesiasticus 25:26.

[73]Matthew 19:4–9 and Mark 10:3–12. The shorter two (Matthew 5:31–2 and Luke 16:18) are of the Q source and are presented as part of public discourses.

[74]Josephus, *Antiquities*, IV, viii:23.

[75]Gunther Bornkamm, *Tradition and Interpretation in Matthew*, G. Barth and H.J. Held, translators (London: SCM, 1963), p. 39.

[76]Matthew 19:4–6; Mark 10:6–9.

[77]Q stands for the German word *quelle*, or "source," and alleged written traditional source of material common to Matthew and Luke.

[78]Josephus, *Antiquities*, XVIII, v: 4; XV, vii: 10; cf. Mark 6:14–29.

[79]For additional indications of the permanence of the marriage bond, Proverbs 18:22 LXX; Ecclus. 7:26; Malachi 2:16. Also a passage in the Damascus Document (VII: 1–3); "The builders of the wall . . . are caught in fornication in two respects; by marrying two women in their lifetime, whereas the principle of creation is 'male and female created he them.'"

2. Prominent Women in Various Apostolic Churches

[1]Acts 1:14–15.

[2]Acts 2:41, 4:4.

[3]Acts 5:1–11; cf. 2:45, 4:32–37.

[4]Acts 12:12ff.

[5]F.F. Bruce, *The Acts of the Apostles* (Grand Rapids MI: Eerdmans, reprinted 1970), pp. 131–136. William Ramsay, *St. Paul the Traveller*, p. 385f.

[6]Isaiah 2:3; Acts 1:8, 8:12, 9:1–2.

[7]Acts 9:32ff.

[8]S.F. Hunter, "Dorcas," *International Standard Bible Encyclopedia*, Vol. II (Grand Rapids MI: Eerdmans, reprinted 1955), p. 870.

[9]Acts 16:1ff.

[10]II Timothy 1:5, 3:15.

[11]Acts 16:12ff.

[12]Homer, *Iliad*, IV, p. 141ff.

[13]Chrysostom, *Homilies on Philippians*, XIII.

[14]Acts 17:1ff.

[15]B.M. Metzger, *A Textual Commentary on the Greek New Testament* (London: United Bible Societies, 1971), p. 453.

[16]Acts 17:10.

[17]R.C.H. Lenski, *The Interpretation of the Acts of the Apostles* (Minneapolis: Augsburg, 1961), p. 703.

[18]Metzger, p. 454; James Hardy Ropes, "The Text of Acts," *The Beginnings of Christianity: Part I, The Acts of the Apostles*, F.J. Foakes Jackson and Kirsopp Lake, editors, Vol. III, p. 162ff; Ramsay, p. 268.

[19]P.H. Menoud, "The Western Text and Theology of Acts," *Bulletin of the Studiorum Novi Testamenti Societies* II (1951), pp. 30ff.

[20]Acts 16:34.

[21]Acts 18:23.

[22]F.F. Bruce, *The Spreading Flame* (Paternoster, 1970), p. 137.

[23]Acts 18:18–19.

[24]A. Robertson and A. Plummer, "First Epistle of St. Paul to the Corinthians," *International Critical Commentary* (Edinburgh: T and T Clark, reprinted 1967), p. 10.

[25]Acts 18:2, 18, and 26.

[26]Metzger, p. 467.

[27]Romans 16:3; II Timothy 4:19; although in I Corinthians 16:19 Aquila is listed first.

[28]Chrysostom, *Homilies on II Timothy*, X.

[29]Bruce, p. 15.

[30]W. Sanday and A.C. Headlam, "The Epistle to the Romans" *International Critical Commentary* (Edinburgh: T and T Clark, reprinted 1968), pp. 418–420.

[31]Romans 16:4.

[32]A. Deissmann, *Light from the Ancient East* (Grand Rapids MI: Baker, 1965), p. 118.

[33]Donald Guthrie, *New Testament Introduction* (Downer's Grove IL: Inter-Varsity, 1973), p. 696f.

[34]Romans 16:1–2.

[35]Acts 6:1–6.

[36]Romans 16:6.

[37]The variant spelling *marian* is to be rejected. United Bible Societies, *The Greek New Testament* (Stuttgart: Württemberg, 1966), p. 574.

[38]Frederic Godet, *Commentary on the Epistle to the Romans* (Grand Rapids MI: Zondervan, reprinted 1969), p. 491.

[39]Romans 16:12.

[40]A. F. Walls, "Tryphena and Tryphosa," *New Bible Dictionary* (London: Inter-Varsity Fellowship, 1962), p. 1302.

[41]Romans 16:8 and 9; I Corinthians 4:17; Ephesians 6:21; Colossians 4:7, 9, and 14; Philemon 2; II Peter 3:15.

[42]Friedrich Hauck, *Theological Dictionary of the New Testament*, G. Kittel, editor, Vol. III (Grand Rapids MI: Eerdmans, 1974), pp. 828–829.

[43]Luke 5:5.

[44]Deissmann, p. 312.

[45]Hauck, pp. 828–829.

[46]Romans 9:3.

[47]Chrysostom, *Homilies on the Acts of the Apostles and the Epistle to the Romans*, XXXI.

[48]C.H. Dodd, "The Epistle of Paul to the Romans," *The Moffatt New Testament Commentary*, James Moffat, editor (New York: Harper and Brothers, 1932), p. 239.

[49]Cf. Acts 14:4 and 14; II Corinthians 8:23; Philippians 2:25.

[50]Lenski, p. 905; C.K. Barrett, *A Commentary on the Epistle to the Romans* (New York: Harper and Row, 1957), p. 283; Sanday and Headlam, p. 423.

[51]Romans 16:13.

[52]F. W. Gingrich, "Rufus," *Interpreter's Dictionary of the Bible*, Vol. IV (New York: Abingdon, 1962), pp. 129–130.

[53]Sanday and Headlam, p. 427.

[54]B.J. Throckmorton, "Claudia," *Interpreter's Dictionary of the Bible*, Vol. I (New York: Abingdon, 1962), p. 640.

[55]*Apostolic Constitutions*, VII, 46 (*ANF*, VII, p. 478); Walter Lock, "The Pastoral Epistles," *International Critical Commentary* (Edinburgh: T and T Clark, 1966), p. 120; Irenaeus, *Against Heresies*, III, 3.

[56]J.B. Lightfoot, *The Apostolic Fathers*, Part I (London Macmillan, 1890), on Clement of Rome, I, pp. 76–79.

[57]Metzger, p. 627; United Bible Societies, p. 703.

[58]J.B. Lightfoot, *Saint Paul's Epistles to the Colossians and Philemon* (Grand Rapids MI: Zondervan, reprinted 1971), pp. 242–243; cf. T.K. Abbott, "Ephesians and Colossians," *International Critical Commentary* (Edinburgh: T and T Clark, reprinted 1968), p. 303.

[59]Colossians 4:9.

[60]Ramsay, *The Church in the Roman Empire*, (London: Hodder and Stoughton, eighth edition, 1904), p. 375; cf. pp. 375–428 for full discussion of the apocryphal work.

[61]W. M. Ramsay, "Asiatic Elements in Greek Civilization," *The Gifford Lectures in the University of Edinburgh, 1915–16* (London: J. Murray, 1928) p. 269.

3. Female Officers in the Early Christian Church

[1]Cf. Acts 20:17, 28, where *episkopos, presbuteros* and the concept of *poimen* are used of a single office, the first officially, and the others descriptively; also I Corinthians 3:5, I Thessalonians 3:2 and Romans 13:4, where *diakonos* is used descriptively of the work of Paul, Apollos, Timothy and secular rulers; also Ephesians 4:11–12 and Acts 6:4, where *diakonia* describes the function of apostles, prophets, evangelists, pastors, and teachers alike.

[2]I Timothy 3:1ff.; Titus 1:5–9.

[3]I Peter 5:1-3; Mark 10:42-43.

[4]Philippians 1:1; I Timothy 3:8-13; possibly also *antilempseis* translated "helps" (I Corinthians 12:28).

[5]Acts 6:8, 8:5-7.

[6]Philippians 1:1.

[7]Romans 16:1.

[8]James H. Moulton and George Milligan, *The Vocabulary of the Greek New Testament* (London: Hodder and Stoughton, 1949), p. 149.

[9]Exodus 38:8; Ezekiel 8:14.

[10]C.H. Dodd, "The Epistle of Paul to the Romans," *The Moffatt New Testament Commentary*, James Moffatt, editor (New York: Harper and Brothers, 1932), p. 235.

[11]II Corinthians 3:6, 6:4; Ephesians 3:7, 6:21; Colossians 1:7, 25 and 4:7; I Timothy 4:6.

[12]Pliny, *Letters*, X, 96.

[13]G.W.H. Lampe, *A Patristic Greek Lexicon* (Oxford: Clarendon, reprinted 1968), p. 353; Clement, *Stromata*, III:6.

[14]Philip Schaff, *History of the Christian Church*, Vol. I (Grand Rapids MI: Eerdmans, reprinted 1968), p. 500.

[15]*Apostolic Constitutions*, III, 3:18-20.

[16]*Apostolic Constitutions*, III, 2:16; VIII, 3:28.

[17]*Apostolic Constitutions*, II, 7:62.

[18]*Apostolic Constitutions*, II, 4:26.

[19]*Apostolic Constitutions*, III, 1:7.

[20]*Apostolic Constitutions*, VII, 2:32.

[21]*Apostolic Constitutions*, VIII, 3:19, 20, 28.

[22]Chrysostom, *Homilies on Timothy*, XI.

[23]Acts 6:1ff.

[24]Chayim Cohen and Ben-Zion Schereschewsky, "Widow," *Encyclopedia Judaica*, Vol. XVI (Jerusalem: Macmillan, 1971), pp. 487-495.

[25]Acts 9:39ff.

[26]Plato, *Laws*.

[27]I Corinthians 7:40; Romans 7:1-3.

[28]I Corinthians 7:8, 9, 39.

[29]R.C.H. Lenski, *The Interpretation of St. Paul's Epistles to the Colossians, to the Thessalonians, to Timothy, to Titus and Philemon* (Minneapolis: Augsburg, 1961), p. 667.

[30]Titus 2:1-5.

[31]Ignatius, "To the Smyrneans," *The Ante-Nicene Fathers*, Vol. I, Alexander Roberts and James Donaldson, editors (Grand Rapids MI: Eerdmans, 1953), p. 92; this longer translation is from the Syriac, whereas the shorter Greek is rendered "and the virgins who are called widows." Such significant differences between the Greek and Syriac texts make the works of Ignatius highly controversial.

[32]Polycarp, *To the Philippians*, 4.

[33]Justin Martyr, *First Apology*, 67.

[34]Lucian, *Death of Peregrinus*, 12.

[35]Tertullian, "On the Veiling of Virgins," 9.

[36]*Apostolic Constitutions*, II, 4, 25.

[37]*Apostolic Constitutions*, II, 26; III, 7; VI, 17.

[38]J.B. Lightfoot, *The Apostolic Fathers*, Part II, Vol. II (London: Macmillan, 1890), p. 322.

[39]Acts 21:9; I Corinthians 7:1-39.

[40]Donald MacKenzie, "Virgin," *Dictionary of the Apostolic Church*, Vol. II (New York: Scribner's, 1919), p. 641.

[41]Justin Martyr, *First Apology*, 15.

[42]Ignatius, "To the Smyrneans."

[43]*Apostolic Constitutions*, II, 25, 26.

[44]*Apostolic Constitutions*, III, 6; IV, 14; VIII, 24.

[45]J.M. Ford,"Levirate Marriage in St. Paul (I Corinthians 7)," *New Testament Studies* 10:3 (April, 1964), p. 361. A. Robertson and A. Plummer, "A Critical and Exegetical Commentary on the First Epistle of Paul to the Corinthians," *International Critical Commentary* (Edinburgh: T and T Clark, second edition, reprinted 1967), p. 135.

[46]Emil Schürer, *A History of the Jewish People in the Time of Christ*, Vol. II, G. Vermes and F. Millar, translators (Edinburgh: T and T Clark, New English edition, 1973), p. 211.

[47]J.M. Ford, "The Meaning of Virgin," *New Testament Studies* 12:3 (April, 1966), pp. 293-299; J.M.Ford, "St. Paul, the Philogamist (I Corinthians vii in Early Patristic Exegesis)," *New Testament Studies* 11:4 (July, 1965), pp. 326-330.

[48]J.K. Elliott, "Paul's Teaching on Marriage in I Corinthians: Some Problems Considered," *New Testament Studies* 19:2 (January, 1973), pp. 219-225.

[49]Plato, *Republic*, VI, 460.

4. Female Leadership in the Early Christian Assembly

[1]Francis Brown, S.R. Driver and C.A. Briggs, editors, *A Hebrew and English Lexicon* (Oxford: Clarendon, reprinted 1968), s.v.

[2]Karl Burger, "Prophecy and the Prophetic Office," *The New Schaff-Herzog Encyclopedia of Religious Knowledge*, Vol. IX, S.M. Jackson, editor (Grand Rapids MI: Baker, reprinted 1964), p. 271; Helmut Kramer, "*Prophetes*," *Theological Dictionary of the New Testament*, Vol. V, Gerhard Friedrich, editor (Grand Rapids MI: Eerdmans, 1971), pp. 786-787.

[3]Exodus 15:20; Numbers 12:2; Judges 4:4; II Kings 22:14; Nehemiah 6:14; Isaiah 8:3.

[4]Luke 2:36.

[5]Gerhard Friedrich, "*Prophetes*," *Theological Dictionary of the New Testament*, Vol. VI, Gerhard Friedrich, editor (Grand Rapids MI: Eerdmans, reprinted 1971), p. 855; Acts 6:6, 8:17-19, 19:6-7.

[6]I Corinthians 14:32.

[7]I Corinthians 14:29; I Thessalonians 5:21; apparently some would attempt to teach the assembly false doctrine, claiming inspiration for authority; cf. I John 4:1.

[8]I Corinthians 14:1, 5; Ephesians 2:20, 3:5, 4:11.

[9]Except possibly in Acts 13:1 and 11:27.

[10]I Corinthians 13:8-13; Ephesians 4:11-16; M.H. Shepherd, "Prophet," *Interpreter's Dictionary of the Bible*, Vol. III (New York: Abingdon, 1962), p. 920; *Theological Dictionary of the New Testament*, p. 850.

[11]I Corinthians 12-14; I Thessalonians 5:11ff.; Ephesians 4:7-13.

[12]I Corinthians 13:9.

[13]W.F. Arndt and W. Gingrich, *A Greek-English Lexicon of the New Testament* (Chicago: The University of Chicago Press, reprinted 1963), s.v. Root of English term "dialogue."

[14]Luke 24:14; Acts 24:26; I Corinthians 15:33.

[15]Ignatius, *Epistle to Polycarp*, V; Justin Martyr, *Dialogue with Trypho* 68:8.

[16]Matthew 5:21, 15:3; Luke 4:16–22.

[17]I Timothy 1:10; II Timothy 4:3; Titus 1:9, 2:1.

[18]Colossians 1:23, 3:16; I Timothy 4:11, 6:2.

[19]Romans 16:14; Ephesians 5:19; I Corinthians 14:15; Hebrews 10:25.

[20]Joel 2:28; Acts 2:17.

[21]Acts 21:7–14, 6:6, 8:5–40.

[22]I Corinthians 11:4–5a

[23]Irenaeus, *Against Heresies*, III, xi, 9.

[24]Tertullian, *Against Marcion*, v, 8.

[25]Chrysostom, *Homily XXIX.*

[26]H.A.W. Meyer, *Critical and Exegetical Handbook to the Epistles to the Corinthians* (New York: Funk and Wagnalls, 1884), p. 247; Abel Isaksson, *Marriage and Ministry in the New Temple; a Study with Special Reference to Matthew 19:3–12 and I Corinthians 11:3–16* (Lund: Gleerup, 1965), p. 155; John Calvin, *Commentary on the Epistles of Paul the Apostle to the Corinthians*, I, 356.

[27]Russel G. Prohl, *Women in the Church, a Restudy of Woman's Place in Building the Kingdom* (Grand Rapids MI: Eerdmans, 1957), p. 30.

[28]Archibald Robertson and Alfred Plummer, "A Critical and Exegetical Commentary on the First Epistle of St. Paul to the Corinthians," *International Critical Commentary* (Edinburgh: T and T Clark, reprinted 1967), pp. 230, 325.

[29]Acts 21:11f., 11:27, 13:1, 15:32.

[30]G.B. Caird, *A Commentary on the Revelation of St. John the Divine* (New York: Harper & Row, 1966), p. 43; cf. I John 2:19, 4:1–3.

[31]Luke 11:1.

[32]H.S. Nash, "Prayer," *New Schaff-Herzog Encyclopedia of Religious Knowledge*, Vol. IX (Grand Rapids MI: Baker, 1964), p. 154.

[33]I Timothy 2:8.

[34]Luke 2:36–38; I Thessalonians 5:17–20; Acts 13:1–3; I Corinthians 14:14–16.

[35]I Samuel 1:13.

[36]Chrysostom, *Homilies on Timothy*, VIII.

[37]W.M. Ramsay, "Historical Commentary on the First Epistle to Timothy," *The Expositor* VIII (September, 1909), p. 274ff. Walter Lock, "A Critical and Exegetical Commentary on the Pastoral Epistles," *International Critical Commentary* (Edinburgh: T and T Clark, reprinted 1966), p. 31.

[38]Karl Heinrich Rengstorf, *"Didasko," The Theological Dictionary of the New Testament*, Vol. II, G. Kittel, editor (Grand Rapids MI: Eerdmans, reprinted 1968), p. 135.

[39]Matthew 4:23, 9:35, 12:9ff., 13:54.

[40]Matthew 13:54; Luke 4:16ff.; Isaiah 61:1ff.

[41]Matthew 5:21ff., 15:3ff., 22:37ff.

[42]Gerhard Friedrich, *"Kerugz," Theological Dictionary of the New Testament*, Vol. III, G. Kittel, editor (Grand Rapids MI: Eerdmans, 1965), p. 703–714.

[43]C.H. Dodd, *The Apostolic Preaching and Its Developments* (London: Hodder and Stoughton, 1944), p. 7.

[44]Acts 2:42, 4:2 and 18, 5:21, 25 and 28; John 14:26; Acts 2:43, 3:1–10, 4:33, 5:12.

[45]F.F. Bruce, *Commentary on the Book of Acts* (Grand Rapids MI: Eerdmans, reprinted 1970), p. 261.

[46]Ernest De Witt Burton, "The Epistle to the Galatians," *International Critical*

Commentary (Edinburgh: T and T Clark, reprinted 1968), p. 335. H. Ridderbos, *The Epistle of Paul to the Churches of Galatia* (Grand Rapids MI: Eerdmans, reprinted 1970), p. 217.

[47]Shepherd of Hermas, *Visions*, III:5.

[48]II Timothy 1:5, 3:14ff.

[49]Titus 2:5ff.

[50]Acts 18:26ff.

[51]W.M. Ramsay, *The Teaching of Paul in Terms of the Present Day* (London: Hodder and Stoughton, 1914), p. 266.

5. Deportment of Women in the Apostolic Church

[1]Oscar Cullmann, *The Early Church*, A.J.B. Higgins, editor (London: SCM, 1956), p. 195.

[2]Romans 12:1ff.; cf. I Corinthians 5:10.

[3]Conrad Arensberg and Arthur Niehoff, *Introducing Social Change* (New York: Aldine-Atherton, 1971), p. 48.

[4]Ephesians 5:25, 28-29.

[5]I Peter 3:7.

[6]Titus 2:4-5; I Corinthians 7:34.

[7]Adolf Deissmann, *Light from the Ancient East* (Grand Rapids MI: Baker, 1965), pp. 314-315.

[8]I Corinthians 7:2-9.

[9]Hebrews 13:4.

[10]Genesis 38:9 undoubtedly refers to *coitus interruptus*.

[11]I Corinthians 7:3-5.

[12]I Corinthians 7:14-16.

[13]I Peter 3:1.

[14]I Corinthians 7:20.

[15]II Corinthians 6:14.

[16]A. Plummer, "Second Epistle of St. Paul to the Corinthians," *International Critical Commentary* (Edinburgh: T and T Clark, reprinted 1966), p. 206.

[17]I Timothy 5:14; Matthew 19:3ff.

[18]I Corinthians 9:5; I Timothy 3:2; 12; Titus 1:6.

[19]I Timothy 4:1ff.

[20]Genesis 2:18-25.

[21]*Genesis Rabbah* 18:2, 45:5.

[22]Ephesians 5:22; Colossians 3:18; I Peter 3:1.

[23]Walter Lock, "The Pastorals," *International Critical Commentary* (Edinburgh: T and T Clark, reprinted 1966), pp. 32-33.

[24]I Corinthians 7:34.

[25]J.H. Moulton and G. Milligan, *The Vocabulary of the Greek Testament* (London: Hodder and Stoughton, reprinted 1963), p. 281.

[26]A.T. Robertson, *Word Pictures in the New Testament*, Vol. IV (New York: Harper and Brothers, 1931), p. 570.

[27]N.J. Hommes, "Let Women Be Silent in the Church; a Message Concerning the Worship Service and the Decorum to Be Observed by Women," *Calvin Theological Journal*, April 1969, pp. 18-19.

[28]James Laver, "Dress," *Encyclopedia Britannica*, Vol. VII (London: William Benton, 1964), pp. 676-677.

[29]Cyprian, *Treatises*, II, 12.

[30]Chrysostom,*Homilies on Timothy*, VIII.

[31]*Apostolic Constitutions*, I, 3:9.

[32]Tertullian, *On the Veiling of Virgins; De Corona*, 4.

[33]Supported by Irenaeus, bishop of Lyons around 190 A.D., *Against Heresies*, VII, 2 (*Ante-Nicene Fathers*, I, p. 327); Clement of Alexandria, 195 A.D., *The Instructor*, III, 11 (*Ante-Nicene Fathers*, II, p. 290); Hippolytus of Rome and Chrysostom of Antioch, both of the fourth century.

[34]Albrecht Oepke, *Theological Dictionary of the New Testament*, Vol. III, G. Kittel, editor (Grand Rapids MI: Eerdmans, 1965), p. 561.

[35]Alfred Plummer, "The First Epistle of St. Paul to the Corinthians," *International Critical Commentary* (New York: Scribner's, 1911), p. 227f.; T.C. Edwards, *A Commentary on the First Epistle to the Corinthians* (London: Hodder and Stoughton, 1885), p. 271; C.K. Barrett, *A Commentary on the First Epistle to the Corinthians* (New York: Harper & Row, 1968), p. 251; R.C.H. Lenski, *The Interpretation of St. Paul's First and Second Epistles to the Corinthians* (Columbus: Lutheran Book Concern, 1946), p. 450.

[36]Genesis 24:65–67.

[37]G. Driver and J. Miles, *The Assyrian Laws* (Oxford: Clarendon, 1935). For a summary of the marriage ceremony and veiling procedure, see J.M. Powis Smith, *The Origin and History of Hebrew Law* (Chicago: University of Chicago Press, 1931), p. 232.

[38]Genesis 38:12, 19.

[39]Roland de Vaux, "Sur le voile des femmes dans l'orient ancien," *Revue Biblique* 44 (1935), p. 408.

[40]Fritz Zerbst, *The Office of Women in the Church: A Study in Practical Theology* (St. Louis: Concordia, 1955), p. 37.

[41]Exodus 28:36–40; Leviticus 8:9.

[42]H.L. Strack and Paul Billerbeck, *Kommentar zum Neuen Testament aus Talmud und Midrash*, Vol. III (Munich: Beck, 1922, reprinted 1970), pp. 423–426. *Babylonian Talmud*, "Shabboth," 13:6.

[43]Plutarch, *Roman Questions, XIV; Moralia* 267B.

[44]Donald Earl, *The Age of Augustus* (New York: Crown, 1968), pp. 75; 92–93.

[45]Jan Lukas, *Pompeii and Herculaneum* (London: Spring, 1966), p. 106.

[46]Virgil, *Aeneid* III, 545.

[47]Plutarch, *Roman Questions*, XIII. Seneca, *Natural Questions*, VII, 3:1.

[48]Dio Chrysostom, *Orations* 33, 48. Plutarch, *Roman Questions*, XIV; *Moralia* 232C.

[49]Macrobius, *Saturnalia*, III, vi 7.

[50]Oepke, p. 562.

[51]Helmut Koster, *Theological Dictionary of the New Testament*, G. Friedrich, editor, Vol, IX (Grand Rapids MI: Eerdmans, 1974), pp. 272–273.

[52]Tertullian, *On the Veiling of Virgins*, VI.

[53]Song of Solomon 4:1, 7:6; Jeremiah 7:29; Deuteronomy 21:12.

[54]Tacitus, *Germania*, 19.

[55]Athenaeus, *The Deipnosophists*, IXX, 27; Aristophanes, *The Thesmophoriazusae*, 838.

[56]C.K. Barrett, p. 251.

[57]Lucian, *Dialogi, Meretricii*, 3; Epictetus, I, xvi, 9–14.

[58]A.T. Robertson, *A Grammar of the Greek New Testament in Light of Historical Research* (Nashville: Broadman, fourth edition, 1934), pp. 809, 948.

[59]A.P. Stanley, *The Epistles of Paul to the Corinthians* (London: John Murray, 1882), p. 179; Hans Conzelmann, *Der Erste Brief an die Korinther* (Gottingen: Vanderhoek and Ruprecht, 1969), p. 212f.; W.E. Vine, *First Corinthians* (London: Oliphants, 1951), p. 146.

[60]Abel Isaksson, *Marriage and Ministry in the New Temple; a Study with Special Reference to Matthew 19:3–12 and I Corinthians 11:3–16* (Lund: Gleerup, 1965), p. 177.

[61]James B. Hurley, "Did Paul Require Veils or the Silence of Women? A Consideraton of I Corinthians 11:2–16 and I Corinthians 14:33b–36," *The Westminster Theological Journal* 35:2 (1973), p. 196.

[62]See the LXX version of Ezekiel 44:18–20; Leviticus 13:45; Numbers 5:18; and Leviticus 10:4–7.

[63]Clement of Alexandria, *Instructor*, XI.

[64]Strack and Billerbeck, p. 427; cf. *Midrash "Ketuboth"* 7:6.

[65]Cullmann, pp. 199–200.

[66]William Hendriksen, *I and II Timothy and Titus* (London: Banner of Truth Trust, reprinted 1964), p. 108.

[67]Matthew 5:16.

[68]I Peter 3:3–4.

[69]*Apostolic Constitutions*, I; 3:9–10.

[70]Dwight Pratt, "Women," *International Standard Bible Encyclopedia*, Vol. V (Grand Rapids MI: Eerdmans, 1939), p. 3103.

6. Equality in Christ

[1]M. Boucher, "Some Unexplored Parallels to I Corinthians 11:11–12 and Galatians 3:28; The New Testament on the Role of Women," *Catholic Biblical Quarterly* 31:50–58 (June, 1969), pp. 57–58.

[2]G.B. Caird, "Paul and Women's Liberty" (Manson Memorial Lecture, University of Manchester, 1971), p. 271.

[3]Galatians 4:22.

[4]Caird, p. 272.

[5]Fritz Zerbst, *The Office of Women in the Church; a Study in Practical Theology* (St. Louis: Concordia, 1955), p. 35.

[6]Romans 10:12; Colossians 3:11; I Corinthians 12:13.

[7]James 1:9–11, 2:1–10.

[8]Philemon; I Peter 2:19; Colossians 3:22.

[9]Romans 13:1ff.; I Peter 2:13ff.

[10]E. De W. Burton, "The Epistle to the Galatians," *International Critical Commentary* (Edinburgh: T and T Clark, reprinted 1968), p. 206; cf. H.N. Ridderbos, *The Epistle of Paul to the Churches of Galatia* (Grand Rapids MI: Eerdmans, reprinted 1970), p. 149.

[11]Henry Chadwick, *The Early Church* (Grand Rapids MI: Eerdmans, 1967), pp. 58–59.

[12]J.B. Lightfoot, *The Epistle of St. Paul to the Galatians* (Grand Rapids MI: Zondervan, reprinted 1972), p. 150; Elisabeth Schüssler Fiorenza, *In Memory of Her* (London: SCM, 1983), pp. 205–241.

[13]Krister Stendahl, *The Bible and the Role of Women: A Case Study in Hermeneutics*, Emilie T. Sanders, translator (Philadelphia: Fortress, 1966), pp. 32–34.

[14]Isaiah 2:1–4.

[15]J.S. Glen, *Pastoral Problems in First Corinthians* (Philadelphia: Westminster, 1964), pp. 137–138.

[16]Caird, p. 281.

[17]Matthew 19:8.

[18]*Genesis Rabbah* 8:9: *Midrash* "Seder Eliahu," 7.

[19]Matthew 19:4–6; I Timothy 2:13–15.

[20]I Timothy 2:13–15.

Index